FIERCE

Women Who Shaped Canada

Lisa Dalrymple

Illustrations by
Willow Dawson

Scholastic Canada Ltd.
Toronto New York London Auckland Sydney
Mexico City New Delhi Hong Kong Buenos Aires

For my mother, Sandie,
and my daughters, Nat and Dani,
who are fierce — L. D.

ᦉ

Scholastic Canada Ltd.
604 King Street West, Toronto, Ontario M5V 1E1, Canada

Scholastic Inc.
557 Broadway, New York, NY 10012, USA

Scholastic Australia Pty Limited
PO Box 579, Gosford, NSW 2250, Australia

Scholastic New Zealand Limited
Private Bag 94407, Botany, Manukau 2163, New Zealand

Scholastic Children's Books
Euston House, 24 Eversholt Street, London NW1 1DB, UK

www.scholastic.ca

Library and Archives Canada Cataloguing in Publication

Dalrymple, Lisa, author
Fierce : women who shaped Canada / Lisa Dalrymple
; illustrated by Willow Dawson.

ISBN 978-1-4431-6382-8 (softcover).--ISBN 978-1-4431-7510-4
(hardcover)

1. Women--Canada--Biography--Juvenile literature.
2. Canada--Biography--Juvenile literature. I. Dawson, Willow,
illustrator II. Title.

FC26.W6D35 2019   j920.720971   C2018-905479-4

Quotes from John Firth's *River Time: Racing the Ghosts of the Klondike Rush* courtesy
of NeWest Press.

6 5 4 3 2 1   Printed in Canada   114   19 20 21 22 23

MIX
Paper from
responsible sources
FSC® C016245
www.fsc.org

Contents

Introduction

Fired by Courage

I wanted to write a book with stories that spoke to me, stories about women that made me think, *Whoa! She really did that?* and *Why haven't I heard about this?* I wanted to write about women like Marguerite de la Roque, who was abandoned by her guardian on a freezing cold island and who survived alone, fighting off wolves and hunting bears; or like Mona Parsons, who helped Allied airmen flee the Nazis before she was caught and sent to a German prison camp, but escaped and then walked barefoot back to the Netherlands; or like Catherine Schubert, who travelled from Manitoba over the Rocky Mountains to British Columbia with her two oldest children in baskets attached to her horse, her toddler often perched on her husband's shoulders, and a baby she delivered after rafting to the shore of the North Thompson River.

In my mind, I didn't necessarily call these women "heroes," which I think of as people acting bravely at a specific moment in time. Rather I thought of them as women who were fired by courage and a rebellious spirit their whole lives. They were *not* the first woman to do something typically done by men, *not* women who disguised their sex in order to take on "manly" roles, but they were women — some of them as young as thirteen — who did things so gruelling, so formidable that it was hard to imagine them being done by anyone.

They were not women I had heard about before — and for a reason. Women have historically lived their lives "off the page," excluded from written documents that are often considered "fact" and thought of as more legitimate than family lore and oral tradition. And stories *told* are more likely to have their "truth" questioned. As well, given that information about Indigenous people and other non-European people in Canada is missing from many historical records, Indigenous and non-European women are doubly hard to find out about.

And so I scoured every document that might include anything about the people in this book, but I also tried to listen to the lore, the oral retellings, the family tales — and to hear their stories. I considered how I came to learn about each woman, and in circumstances where details were missing, I asked myself what we don't know and why we can't know it.

There are some cases in which I could find out very little about a particular woman; her voice came to me as no more than a whisper. What spoke to me instead was a similarity or connection between her and another woman. These became *Sister Stories,* the stories about Charlotte Small, Lucile Hunter and Joan Bamford Fletcher. Because even though these women weren't included in many records and journals, their lives were meaningful. It's important to know that, at every moment in history, somewhere near you, there were inspiring women surviving incredible challenges.

This is the book I wanted to write, the stories that spoke to me, but these women are not the only ones fired by courage and a rebellious spirit. Women live unheralded lives like this all the time. And they are *Fierce.*

~ Lisa Dalrymple

Alone Among Demons

Marguerite de la Roque
July 1542
An island in the Gulf of Saint Lawrence

Marguerite glared at her guardian, Captain Jean-François de Roberval, Viceroy of Canada. At his orders, two sailors hauled ashore everything that she had brought with her to the New World. Then, as though in some final insult, they unloaded four arquebuses and ammunition — as if Marguerite or her maidservant knew how to use the nine-kilogram weapons!

Captain Roberval grinned, fully aware that the two women had no chance against the wild animals on this uncharted island of rock, never mind the fiends and monsters the fishermen had warned his crew about.

"Enjoy your exile on *l'Île des Démons!*" he said.

From the nearest ship, Marguerite heard a call. She watched as one of the men shouldered his firearm and forced his way through the sailors to a second rowboat.

She felt the bones of her corset as it tightened around her ribs. Why would he want to share their death sentence? Yet as the young man reached the shore, Marguerite ran to him crying, "*Mon cheri!*"

Captain Roberval, looking quite satisfied, stepped into his boat and was rowed back to the ship. Marguerite waited for the sailors to protest. Surely they could make him change his mind. But she had been foolish. She had been seen walking alone with the young man on the hills around St. John's, Newfoundland, and making nighttime visits to his cabin. Roberval claimed that if anyone were to hear of it, their family name would be ruined — and her guardian's wrath was too well known for any of the sailors to challenge him.

Watching the ships, the *Sainte Anne*, the *Vallentyne* and the *Marye*, sail from the harbour, Marguerite leaned against her suitor. Though it was July, the sea spray chilled everything it touched. Her elderly maidservant, Damienne, shivered. They needed a fire before nightfall.

Marguerite and Damienne collected wood and checked the rock pools for fresh water while the young man built a lean-to with the canvas that he had brought from the ship. Convinced that he could signal a fishing boat, he lit a signal fire and insisted they keep it burning at all times.

But as their first night closed in, Marguerite's mind reeled at the dangers around them. To raise her spirits, her suitor pulled out his citre, the stringed instrument that he had brought with him on the voyage. He played a few tunes from the rural south of France, their home.

Perhaps it was the music that attracted the creatures, as soon Marguerite saw a pair of glowing yellow eyes in the darkness. They were joined by another pair and then another.

The young man fired his arquebus, and the eyes disappeared. But Marguerite heard a menacing growl from the woods. Beast or demon, she did not know. While her suitor measured out a fresh charge for the gun and hurried to adjust the wick, she searched for rocks. She threw stones into the woods while he fired. Together they fought off the creatures until the sun reappeared above the horizon.

On the second night, the beasts grew braver, scratching at the lean-to. All around them the castaways heard demonic cries, like the insane laughter of a hundred thousand men. Damienne read aloud from the Bible. The louder the prayers, the quieter the creatures' howls — as if they were being driven away.

The next morning the young man began work on a small shelter made from driftwood and the scrawny trees on the island. Searching for long, straight branches, Marguerite found a dead creature that looked like some sort of hound. From the wound in its side, she could tell that it had been killed by one of the shots fired in the night. Looking at the beast's sharp fangs and massive claws, she wondered how a cabin of branches could ever protect them.

The summer passed and the castaways ate berries, mushrooms, fish and meat. Marguerite and her young man married in a ritual of word and gift with Damienne as a witness. The young husband presented his wife with a bed of cedar boughs covered in the furs of animals that they had hunted. When she realized she was pregnant, Marguerite's heart filled with hope: they would be rescued, return to France, and become a true family with Damienne as their nursemaid.

As the thought of the child growing inside her brought Marguerite strength, her husband's spirits began to fade. He had kept his lookout every day but he had not seen a single ship. The winds of winter gusted through the walls of the shelter. The castaways' prayers kept the demons at bay but not the voracious animals that clawed at the cabin each night.

One day the young man said that they should let the signal fire burn out to conserve wood. Marguerite knew him well enough now to know that he feared the worst. She tried to give him hope, talking endlessly about their baby who would be born within the month. Damienne attempted to entice him with new meals created from their meagre ingredients. Both women reassured him that fishing boats would return in the spring. But in February,

1543, after months of drinking water from rock pools and eating whatever food they could find, the young man's belly bloated and he became feverish. With no strength left to fight, Marguerite's new husband died. She and Damienne dug a grave for him as deep as they could in the frozen soil.

The bears and wolves were attracted by the smell of fresh meat. Their attacks became more frequent and frenzied. Marguerite took up watch each night, using her husband's gun to drive the beasts from his grave.

Then finally her baby came — her treasure. Marguerite cut linen from her underskirts to use as swaddling clothes and carried him under her fur cape. She and Damienne baptized him, but they struggled to keep him safe when his cries seemed to beckon the starving beasts. Frightened, cold and aching with hunger, Marguerite defended her small family. There was no time to cry for her husband.

When it seemed to Marguerite that things could not get bleaker, spring returned to the island. The baby loved watching the partridges that walked right into the shelter. Damienne preferred collecting their eggs. She foraged for mushrooms and fished while Marguerite hiked across the island with a readied arquebus under each arm — one to provide her first shot and one for quick backup. It was not unusual for her to kill a caribou or a bear.

One morning, after having killed two bears, she looked

up to see a third above her on a granite outcrop — its hide was as white as snow. The bear charged toward Marguerite. She raised her gun and pulled the lever. As the ball tore into the bear's shoulder, the creature roared. Its foreleg collapsed and it toppled forward. Marguerite took a step closer and aimed her second arquebus. She fired to kill.

Bear meat was foul-tasting, but Marguerite knew that she had to dry as much as possible. She could not last through another winter of starvation, frozen to near death and no energy to even chop wood — not with a child to provide for. She told Damienne that they should start drying berries and she wanted to fortify the cabin's walls with peat. Damienne, who was usually so helpful, simply nodded.

During some of the previous winter's storms, the castaways had hidden out in a cave at the north end of the island. It had been too small for three adults, but two could slide down into it and seal off its entrances with hides.

"Do you think that it would be warmer for the baby in the cave?" Marguerite asked Damienne.

Again Damienne was silent. She had a look Marguerite had only seen once — in the eyes of her husband before he died. Not long after this, Marguerite found Damienne's body at the bottom of a bluff. Perhaps the wind had caught her skirts and blown her from the top.

With no one to help her, Marguerite dug a fresh grave alongside her husband's. That night she guarded their resting site alone — as she would be now in everything that she did.

When dawn arrived, Marguerite thought that she had never witnessed a sun that brought with it so little heat. Her son began to cry and Marguerite resigned to press on.

"Come, *mon trésor*," she said as she strapped him to her back and returned to collecting water, chopping wood and hunting. Carrying the baby, she could only take one arquebus so she tied her husband's old sword around her waist.

But all her efforts could not ensure the survival of her

child. A month after she had buried Damienne, Marguerite cradled another body in her arms. Laying her treasure to rest beside his father, she wept beside his tiny grave.

The beasts sensed that Marguerite was now alone. The demonic cries she had not heard since those first nights returned. As she guarded her small cemetery, her gunpowder now stale and useless, Marguerite was haunted by the thought that when she died, there would be no one to bury her.

She descended into madness and could no longer tell vision from reality. Dressed in skins, she became as wild as the animals that clamoured to devour her. Later Marguerite would not talk about these months, except to tell of a pack of growling beasts that ambushed her one day. Using only her battered sword, she fought off one after another, killing four as she scrambled her way back to the cabin.

As her third winter was closing in, a fishing ship sailed onto the horizon. Marguerite, uncertain if this was a hallucination, ran along the shoreline waving furs in the air. To the fishermen she looked like one of the demons said to haunt the island. Watching to make sure that they did not vanish, Marguerite lit the signal fire and sent up thick smoke. The ship ventured closer.

When the fishermen landed, they were shocked to find one of their countrywomen stranded on this harsh and

remote island. It had been two years and five months. They offered her passage back to France — and Marguerite's heart tore in two. To return home she had to leave the island where she had buried the three people she most loved.

But to stay would give Roberval the satisfaction of knowing she eventually died where he had exiled her. She boarded the ship and sailed back to France, where she quietly carried with her the story that marks her as Canada's first French settler. Yet few people have even heard her name.

How Do We Know What We Know?

Marguerite told her story to André Thevet, a Catholic clergyman who wrote about her many years after she returned to France. She was careful about what details she shared — especially since Thevet would not have approved of her Protestantism or her relationship with the young man. Another version of the tale was told by queen Marguerite de Navarre. But the queen wrote the story as she was told it by Captain Roberval, and André Thevet was a close friend of the Captain. Both accounts are likely influenced by her guardian's perspective.

What Do We Know?

Roberval was the Viceroy of Canada, one of the five colonies of New France, which is why we know who he was. His name was *Jean-François de la Rocque*, but he preferred to be known by his title, *Sieur de Roberval.*

Some say that the Isle of Demons, where Roberval abandoned Marguerite, is Quirpon Island off the coast of Newfoundland. But Elizabeth Boyer, in her book *A Colony of One*, writes that it is Hospital Island, one of the Harrington Islands that are now a part of Quebec. Roberval, having heard folk tales about islands populated by horned fiends and monsters, tried to scare the castaways by calling the place *l'Île des Démons.* The island was known by this name for a while.

What Don't We Know?

We don't actually know who Marguerite was. She may have been Roberval's sister, niece, cousin or cousin once removed. Marguerite was a very popular name in France at that time and there were also many De la Rocques/Roques. We only know that this Marguerite was a close relation of Roberval's and that her parents were probably dead, which is why she would have required the protection of a male relative. We don't know how old she was — both unmarried women and children required guardians or chaperones at that time.

We don't know the identity of her suitor. Thevet said that he had come along on the ship because he loved Marguerite, so he must have been someone she already knew before the journey. He was probably a nobleman if he had a musical instrument like a citre with him. His sword and arquebus suggest he likely had some military training.

Upon his return to France, Roberval — not wanting to anger a noble family — made sure that the story of the marooning was shrouded in secrecy. Even the passenger list for the voyage somehow disappeared. If the fishermen had not come across Marguerite's island, no one would have heard any more about her. The story that Roberval almost succeeded in burying is the story of Canada's first French settler. But in history books, the names of Cartier, Champlain and Roberval are the ones you are much more likely to find.

In Pursuit of Peace

Ttha'naltther

Spring 1713
Denedeh or Present-Day Northern Manitoba

For a long time, the Nehiyawak and the Dene had been at war. Thousands of people, young and old, had been killed. By 1713, when Ttha'naltther's Dene village was attacked, the Nehiyawak had acquired guns from their trade with the Europeans. This gave them a huge advantage in their war with the Dene, and many of Ttha'naltther's relatives were killed. But because Ttha'naltther was strong and beautiful, the raiders realized that she would be valuable as a slave of war and potential wife. They took her prisoner instead. She was probably no older than sixteen.

A year and a half passed and Ttha'naltther worked hard for her master. But she did not intend to be a slave forever. She studied life around camp and she listened; she began to understand the language; she observed her captors' use of guns for hunting and warfare; she used pots and kettles, items that were unfamiliar to her people; and she learned that all these things had been traded by the *tthot'né* or "stone house men," the Europeans who lived in forts.

In the fall, when her captors moved camp, Ttha'naltther and another Dene woman seized their chance to escape. Not far to the south of the Nehiyaw camp was the fort of the *tthot'né* — sometimes they could hear their guns. But the women headed north, desperate to get back to their own country before winter. They stayed in one spot only long enough to snare a rabbit or a ptarmigan. But the weather soon turned colder, the rabbits and ptarmigans grew scarce, and edible berries and lichen became harder to find. Ttha'naltther and her friend knew their only chance for survival was to turn back toward the fort, back in the direction of their captors.

It was now the middle of November and the snow was deep. While Ttha'naltther's resolve to reach safety remained strong, the other woman instead grew weak. The hunger and cold were too much to bear. Only five days before Ttha'naltther found a camp of the fort's goose hunters, her friend died. Alone, Ttha'naltther tracked the hunters to their tents and approached them speaking in the broken Nehiyawewin she hoped they would understand. The hunters gave her food and took her back to York Fort, where she was introduced to James Knight, the

Hudson Bay Company (HBC) officer who was the governor there.

Knight offered Ttha'naltther shelter while she recovered and he asked her many questions — about the furs her people could trade for goods, about their access to copper and gold and about passage to the west of the continent. But Ttha'naltther had seen the Nehiyawak camped around the fort and she was suspicious of a man who surrounded himself with her people's enemies. Ttha'naltther wanted Knight to know what the Nehiyawak had done to her people.

"They attack our villages. They have killed many of my relations. They take women as slaves," she told him.

She thought Knight seemed upset, but she could also

see how valuable her people's furs and "yellow metals" were to him. She knew that their war with the Nehiyawak — who lived in the country between the fort and the Dene — was standing in his way.

Over the winter, Ttha'naltther learned some English and Knight wrote about her in the York Fort journal, calling her "Slave Woman Joan" or, more often, just "the Slave Woman." Ttha'naltther and Knight talked about the best way for her to return to her people, negotiate peace between them and the Nehiyawak and establish trade with the HBC.

In the spring of 1715, Ttha'naltther intended to leave the fort for the north. A Nehiyaw chief called Wapasu, who Knight called "Captain" in the journal, volunteered to lead an expedition of his people to take her home and establish a treaty. Knight threw huge feasts for the Nehiyawak. He presented them with gifts, promised rewards to anyone who would accompany Ttha'naltther and concluded his ceremony by passing around a pipe. In all, 150 Nehiyaw men, women and children joined the peace expedition. Knight assigned one of his men, William Stewart, as an HBC representative. He gave him and Ttha'naltther gifts for the Dene and commissioned Stewart to protect Ttha'naltther and her people.

Dene stories tell that Ttha'naltther set out in red cloth given to her by Knight, and York Fort accounts show that she was given a pound of beads. She would have been able to stitch a coat or hood that would identify her as Dene when she approached any camps that they came across. She carried with her a fancy blanket from the HBC fort and a shiny kettle that Knight had given her as a gift.

Living among the Nehiyawak again was a struggle for Ttha'naltther. Determined to show them that they did not scare her, she often told them that they were cowards for the way their people had killed hers. Stewart was afraid that his job of protecting her would become a challenge.

Ttha'naltther knew the journey home would be difficult, particularly when it came to crossing the northern Barrens where food and firewood were scarce. But the hardships began earlier. Not long after they left, a sickness spread among the expedition members, making it impossible to travel quickly. Within the first few weeks of their journey, entire families were forced to turn back.

It took the expedition two months just to get to Churchill River, and Ttha'naltther feared that they were out of rhythm with the seasons. It was already the end of August and, this far north, winter would be closing in soon. As they crossed the Churchill and turned to head northwest, Ttha'naltther could not have known that there were still seventeen rivers between her and home.

By the time that they arrived in the Barrens, it was late in the year and the animals had already moved on, along with the people who followed them. There would also be no more trees — and no fires for cooking or heat — until they crossed ten more rivers and reached the wooded area on the other side. Already weakened, the travellers now faced hunger and cold.

Ttha'naltther turned to the land to find strength to keep moving. She knew how to survive on lichen, but as the weather turned worse even that was soon covered in drifts of snow that towered 2 metres high. The wind erased all signs of tracks as soon as the travellers passed. If anyone strayed from the single-file line they walked in, they risked being lost completely.

Ttha'naltther's pack was heavy, and although she knew Knight wanted her to take gifts to the Dene, there was no point in carrying so many tools and pots if she died before she could deliver them. Eventually she and Stewart threw away a great many of the heavier items.

The winter was colder than any that Ttha'naltther remembered. Some days it was impossible to leave the tents, never mind take them down and move forward. And although many had already turned back, the group was still too large to feed. They had exhausted what provisions they had brought, and some of Chief Wapasu's followers had even resorted to eating their dogs.

When they had gone eight days without food, he called his people around. They had to break into smaller groups. Many of them turned back toward York Fort, but Ttha'naltther, Chief Wapasu, Stewart and a few other people would continue forward. Another group of eight strong men would take a different route and continue north. They were also committed to making peace with the Dene.

In the six weeks since they had crossed the Churchill River, the expedition had covered only 160 kilometres. For six more weeks they continued through the Barrens, but the prolonged hunger took its toll. Then some new sickness descended. Chief Wapasu was one of five who fell seriously ill. Stewart looked wild and began rambling that their captain was going to die and they would all starve to death in the middle of nowhere. But Ttha'naltther was determined to be strong. The land would guide her to the end of the Barrens and to the woods beyond where the animals had gone for shelter.

As the good hunting grounds came within reach, Chief Wapasu sent out two of his fittest hunters. They returned with enough fresh meat for everyone. Now with food to eat and wood for fire, the sick and starving feasted. But food after such deprivation only made them sicker. The two hunters went out again, arranging to meet them farther along the way. But they never did.

One day in February, seven months since the expedition had left York Fort, they finally came across tracks

— Dene tracks, not like those made by the rounded snowshoes of the Nehiyawak. Ttha'naltther knew she was in home territory and that the people ahead were Dene. Wanting them to see her before the group of Nehiyaw strangers, she took the lead. Ttha'naltther could smell the smoke from her people's fires, and the tops of their tents soon came into sight. She pushed forward, calling out in her own language for the first time in more than a year. But there was no response.

As she came into the camp, Ttha'naltther understood why. The snow was stained with blood, and bodies were strewn on the ground. They had been shot. Ttha'naltther turned on Chief Wapasu and his followers. Nine of her people lay around them in the snow and she was certain the group of eight men who had taken a different route were responsible.

Chief Wapasu assured Ttha'naltther those men would never have done this, but he was not so sure. He was also nervous. Tracks in the snow revealed that some Dene had escaped. And now he had brought his group of Nehiyawak right to the scene of a massacre in the heart of Dene territory. He was sure that Ttha'naltther's people would want revenge. The expedition could not go on. Seeing Ttha'naltther's fury and hearing Chief Wapasu's fears, Stewart agreed.

Ttha'naltther knew there were tensions between her

people and the Nehiyawak — deep hatred, fears and anger — but that was exactly what the expedition had been intended to resolve. She understood that the Nehiyawak did not want to continue, but she would not turn back until she had delivered Knight's message to her people. Ttha'naltther would journey on alone, following the tracks of those who had escaped, and return with her Dene relations.

She gathered her fancy blanket, a knife, some matches and her shiny kettle along with what provisions they could spare and the few gifts she still had. As she set out alone, she asked Chief Wapasu and Stewart to give her more time.

"Wait here for ten days before you return to York Fort without me," Ttha'naltther said. She left them fortifying their camp with a fence of wooden stakes and loopholes they could fire through.

Ttha'naltther walked through the dark woods and the snow, now only needing to concern herself with her own energy and pace. She trusted in the spirit of the land and focussed on what might be just out of sight.

Before she could see them, Ttha'naltther heard the large gathering of Dene. As she came through the woods, she saw at least one hundred tents. She marched into the camp, and as soon as she stopped walking, Ttha'naltther began talking. She knew the Nehiyawak and Stewart would be returning to York Fort soon.

She told the Dene that they were not the same Nehiyawak as had been raiding their camps. She explained that Chief Wapasu and his followers had come for peace and endured great hardship to achieve it. She distributed her gifts, lit a fire with matches, made tea in her shiny kettle, and told her people about the Englishmen who wanted to trade with them. For days she answered questions. She argued. She debated. She lectured. She talked herself hoarse. She beseeched her people to make peace with the Nehiyawak. She spoke until many were nodding. They wanted to go with her to see the *tthot'né*.

One hundred sixty men followed Ttha'naltther back to where she had left the others. Exactly ten days after she had set out on her own, she approached the camp and saw the Nehiyawak preparing to leave. She rushed forward, waving and calling out. When Stewart saw her, Ttha'naltther approached with only two Dene representatives. Oral tradition describes how she was placed on a platform and that, as she watched the rest of her people gather around, she sang with joy.

Now face-to-face, the Nehiyawak and the Dene became cautious once again. Ttha'naltther reminded her people that these were not the Nehiyawak responsible for the attacks and, this time, she scolded and argued with both sides. Ttha'naltther persuaded and pushed and reminded them why they had come, making them all stand in fear. By the time the sacred pipe was passed around, not one person — Nehiyawak, Dene or English — refused it.

For the next two days, the large party camped together, exchanging gifts and adopting sons from one group to another, a tradition that symbolized peace. Ttha'naltther passed among her relations, arranging for ten men, women and children to travel back with her to York Fort. She chose carefully. One man who had been adopted by Chief Wapasu was the son of the "greatest traveller in the country." Another man became Ttha'naltther's husband.

The return, while not as perilous, still took them sixty days. It was May 7, 1716, more than ten months since she had left the previous summer, when Ttha'naltther and Stewart returned to York Fort with her delegation of

Nehiyawak and Dene. She was triumphant and Knight was thrilled. He recorded in the journal that, even though the expedition members had suffered hunger, cold and great hardships, their journey had been successful. He credited the "Slave Woman" as the main person responsible. Ttha'naltther resumed her role as Knight's advisor and commanded respect from everyone at the fort.

She remained furious with the eight men who had killed the Dene they had found in the camp. Upon the men's return to York Fort, they had explained what had happened: the Dene, realizing they were being tracked by a party of Nehiyawak, had attacked first. But Ttha'naltther persisted in reminding the Nehiyawak of the slaughter.

Even her own people were cautious of her. When an older Dene man suggested that he would trade poor quality skins to the Englishmen, Ttha'naltther called him a fool. She grabbed his nose, pushed him backwards, and warned him that he should do nothing to jeopardize the trade. Not even Knight was safe. He wrote in the journal about her "devilish spirit," a passion the like of which he had never seen before.

Knight intended to send Ttha'naltther and four other Dene north again that winter. Ttha'naltther disagreed. She was determined to help him establish a post where he could trade with her people, but she would not set out again until the following spring. However, it was a long, hard winter and there were no fresh provisions at York Fort. When an illness broke out, taking hold of Ttha'naltther and some of the other Dene, the fort's doctor did not know how to treat them. All the medicines he had brought had spoiled. Knight took Ttha'naltther and a boy into his own quarters to care for them. But there was little he could do either.

Ttha'naltther died on February 5, 1717. Knight was devastated. He recorded in the fort's journal that, despite the beautiful weather, he was "most melancholy by the loss of her." He buried her, along with the other Dene who died at the fort, in a nearby graveyard that has since been swallowed by the Hayes River.

The agreement Ttha'naltther established between the Nehiyawak and the Dene was a significant step on the two nations' road to peace. To this day, she is remembered as The Peacemaker. In 2017, 300 years after Ttha'naltther's death, a plaque honouring her was unveiled in Churchill, Manitoba, near the site of the trading post Knight established only months after she died.

How Do We Know
What We Know?

Ttha´naltther's story is part of the Dene oral tradition, which is spoken, not written down. In oral storytelling, both the words uttered and the method of telling are important. We can study Émile Petitot's written versions of the Ttha´naltther story from the 1880s and the story Edward Curtis published in 1920, but these men *wrote down* the stories they were *told* and they also brought to them their own non-Indigenous worldview.

The York Fort journals provide dates and other details. In them Governor Knight includes some information about Ttha´naltther, but he mainly focusses on the business of the fort.

What Do We Know?

We know that Ttha´naltther was born between 1697 and 1700. She may have been only thirteen when she was captured by a Nehiyaw raiding party and as young as sixteen or seventeen when she negotiated peace between the Nehiyawak and Dene.

Ttha´naltther was so committed to establishing a trading post on the Churchill River that she planned to journey north again even if her new husband refused to go with her. When she realized that she was dying, she asked to speak to the young Englishman who would have accompanied her. She passed on to him as much as she could of her language and knowledge and reassured him that he should undertake the journey without her. She never made it to Churchill, Manitoba,

the place where there is now a plaque that honours her as a "Person of National Historic Significance."

What Don't We Know?

Many Dene communities claim Ttha´naltther as their own but because there is no map of her route home, we don't know for certain where she was from. She may have been Denesuline or Tlicho or a member of another Dene nation. There are also many variations of her name. Edward Curtis recorded it as Thanádĕlthŭr and so, in many written accounts, she is referred to as Thanadelthur. Denesuline elders used the name Ttha´naltther when they shared their knowledge with Lorraine Hoffman-Mercredi and Phillip Coutu for their book *Inkonze: The Stones of Traditional Knowledge.*

History recorded by non-Indigenous communities has typically valued the written word over oral tradition. James Knight rarely acknowledged individual Nehiyawak or Dene people in his written accounts. What little he did record was usually from the perspective of how different groups of Indigenous people could help him. His accounts were subject to cultural misunderstandings and very often they would have come to him through the words of an interpreter. The story of Ttha´naltther is difficult to learn through online or written resources. To understand it, we must reflect on the invaluable knowledge and memories of the Dene elders passed down through oral storytelling.

A Family Stays Together

Catherine Schubert

May 1862
Fort Garry (present-day Winnipeg, Manitoba)

If Augustus thought Catherine would wait in Fort Garry while he lit out for the goldfields of the Cariboo, he would soon see how wrong he was.

Meeting his eyes, Catherine stated, "A family stays together."

But Augustus Schubert's plans were made. A group of men led by Thomas McMicking had arrived in Fort Garry all the way from Niagara Falls. They planned to travel across the prairies and over the Rocky Mountains to the goldfields of British Columbia, and Augustus intended to join them.

"I'll send for you when I've staked my claim," he declared. "And that's what it is."

Gold fever had made Augustus downright unreasonable. It was useless for Catherine to point out that he would be leaving her alone with the family store, the farm and three young children, just as it was futile to argue that she was not afraid of hardship.

She had starved in Ireland's Great Famine before boarding a ship to the New World as a young teenager, leaving her parents and eight older siblings behind; taught herself to read while working as a maid to send money back home; and fled the frontier violence of Saint Paul, Minnesota, with Augustus and their three babies. There was no reason that Catherine could not journey more than 5600 kilometres, braving the wilderness and crossing the Rocky Mountains — even if she would be the only woman among 150 men.

Instead of debating, Catherine smoothed down the front of her full skirts, reminding Augustus of their fourth child now in her belly, and repeated, "But a family stays together. And that's what it is."

A week later, when Augustus arrived at Long Lake, a three-day walk from Fort Garry, Catherine was beside him, two basket cradles slung across the back of her horse. In one she carried four-year-old Mary Jane and in the other six-year-old Gus. Little Jimmy perched on his father's shoulders as Augustus led the ox and black cow that pulled their covered wagon packed with clothes, bedding, mining tools, herbs, flour and dried meat. Catherine was ready for anything.

Before setting out on the morning of June 5, 1862, "the Overlanders" held a meeting. Each of the many groups — some from as far away as New York and Quebec, but most from cities or small towns in Ontario — appointed a leader to represent them. They agreed that they would walk ten hours each day, that they would rest on Sundays, and that McMicking would negotiate all interactions with the Indigenous people they would meet. After lunch, the expedition set out in a procession of ninety-seven large two-wheeled Red River carts.

They were led by a Métis guide named Charles Racette. There was also a doctor in the group, for which Catherine was grateful. She was certain she would not need him herself — the journey was expected to take two months, and her baby was due in four — but it was reassuring to have him there for her children.

Each day the Overlanders travelled around 35 kilometres. Catherine would wake before 4 a.m., set water to boil, prepare breakfast and get her children up, fed and toileted. She loved mornings. When the 5 a.m. call "Every man to his ox!" came, she would take a moment to stretch her stiff back and amuse herself with the scene around her. Men would be running with cups of tea in one hand and pancakes in the other. Mr. Morrow had a particularly stubborn ox; as he yoked it, the animal would jump, bellow, thrash and throw itself down.

Catherine caught Augustus laughing. "No wonder the fool beast's name is Buck!"

"Augustus!" She swatted him but could not help how her own lips twitched into a smirk.

The Overlanders stopped for the night around 6 p.m. Catherine lit a fire, strained water from the nearest pool — usually ripe with dead plants and animal matter — and set it to boil. She prepared supper; laid buffalo robes in the tent; baked bannock for the next day; started laundry for her family and others; and tended to Gus, Mary Jane and Jimmy. She relished the evenings, when the men gathered with flutes and fiddles, the older children danced and Jimmy threw his arms in the air and ran around them.

Crossing the prairies was more challenging than the Overlanders had imagined. With no roads and no maps to serve them, they were completely dependent on Racette. They were swarmed by biting insects and endured scorching prairie heat. Some days they walked hours between water sources. Catherine was grateful that their old black cow provided milk for her children. At the same time, the nights were so cold that even in June she woke to find ice on her kettle and frost on the ground, which meant that the animals could not graze.

The morning of June 18, Racette did not arrive to lead the expedition. The Overlanders set out thinking that he would catch up, but by nightfall it was obvious that he was not coming back. McMicking recorded in his diary that this was his worst fear: they were in the middle of the prairie without a guide. But the men determined to travel on alone, changing the schedule to begin walking at 3 a.m. and breaking for breakfast when it was warm enough to have melted the frost on the grass.

There was only one time on the journey that Catherine's courage completely failed her. On June 30, when crossing the South Saskatchewan River, a man named Kelso was swept away, his head pulled underwater. After three other men dove beneath the surging waters to retrieve his limp body, Catherine watched Dr. Stevenson work to revive him. Her legs gave out, and she sat down on the riverbank and sobbed.

Still, it was moments like these that won her the men's respect. On the bank of the South Saskatchewan, Catherine pulled herself together and stood up. She gathered her children and helped to ferry them across the river, consoling them as they cried and offering a prayer of thanks when everyone passed unharmed.

By July 1 the expedition had travelled 800 kilometres. They arrived at Fort Carlton just as Indigenous hunters brought in fresh buffalo meat to be dried and made into pemmican for the Hudson Bay Company forts. Catherine and her family were grateful for something different to eat. As they continued on from Fort Carlton, a pack of wolves began tracking them, growing nearer every night. One morning a man shot a large one very close to their camp. At night Catherine's sleep was restless and she found that she did not mind getting up at 2:30 a.m. for the earlier start.

At this time they were also plagued by eleven solid days of rain, during which streams swelled into raging torrents, and Catherine's horse waded through water so deep it flooded Gus and Mary Jane's baskets. With no sun and no way to light a fire, everything was drenched. At night Augustus pitched their tent on top of brush that he piled

in 10 centimetres of water. It was July 21 by the time the Overlanders camped outside Fort Edmonton (present-day Edmonton, Alberta) — and seven weeks since they had left Fort Garry.

The next morning dawned beautiful and bright. The Overlanders laundered their clothes and dried them in the sun. They stayed in the area for over a week, consulting with people who knew their route and hiring André Cardinal, a Métis guide who would take them as far as Tête Jaune Cache in the Rocky Mountains. They sold the Red River carts, which would be useless in the mountains, and purchased packhorses. Having been told that it was unsafe to cross the Rockies so late in the year and also that there was gold in the streams around Fort Edmonton, twenty-five of the men decided to stay. Catherine hoped Augustus would do the same.

Augustus had similar hopes for Catherine. She liked the village of Lac Ste. Anne, not far from Fort Edmonton, where she bought potatoes, berries, butter and gifts for the children. There were nuns at the mission there, and she was happy to have other women to talk to. As she was now more than six months pregnant, Augustus suggested she stay and he would send for her in the spring.

Catherine shook her head. "A family stays together."

They left Lac Ste. Anne on August 2. In the next few days there were several injuries: Catherine's horse reared back, hitting her in the head and knocking out one of her teeth; Mr. Morrow had to return to the village after he was trampled by his ox; and at McLeod's River, Cardinal had to save at least one man from drowning in the current.

Forests replaced the prairies and progress was painfully slow, especially through the waist-deep bogs of stinking mud that dragged against Catherine's skirts. Around her, horses thrashed and panicked, causing them to sink deeper. Many had to be rescued. Some were left to die.

A work party forged ahead to clear brush and fallen trees, but still the trail was too narrow for the children to ride in their baskets. Catherine let Gus ride her horse while she carried Mary Jane on her back and one of the men carried Jimmy. Catherine's entire body ached. The nights grew colder although it was only August. How long would it be before winter set in? She wondered if they would make it to the Cariboo before her baby was born. She was now seven months pregnant.

Then after two weeks of trudging through bogs, Catherine emerged from a thick forest to see the Rocky Mountains before her. Though still 160 kilometres away, their very presence beckoned the travellers along the Athabasca River. Food stocks had become so low that the men hunted even on Sunday. They were relieved to meet Métis hunters who sold them two mountain sheep. Finally on August 18, the weary trekkers arrived at the base of Roche Miette.

Everyone believed that the Cariboo was close.

The next morning they headed up to Disaster Point, where the path narrowed to a 30-centimetre-wide ledge with a rock wall on one side and a 400-metre drop on the other. When it was Catherine's turn to cross, she placed her back against the cold rock and crept along, trying to account for the additional weight in her belly. She told Gus and Mary Jane to crawl, but when word came back that two horses had plunged over the edge, she instead made them lie down. Short of breath in the thin mountain air, Catherine coaxed her children along, trying to quell her panic as they wriggled across on their bellies.

They passed Jasper House, where they had expected to purchase fresh provisions, but found it closed. The Overlanders had to kill their first ox. In the next nine days they would eat porcupine, skunk, lichen soup and even one of their horses. On August 22 they made it to the Great Divide, the ridge of the Rocky Mountains that marks the entry into British Columbia. To the west was the headwaters of the Fraser River, which they knew would lead them to the Cariboo. Five days later, the Overlanders arrived at the Secwepemc camp at Tête Jaune Cache, and gratefully traded with the villagers for their dried mutton, berry cakes and freshly-caught salmon.

The Overlanders stayed at Tête Jaune Cache for a few days, during which time they consulted with Secwepemc hunters on the best route to the Cariboo. Knowing the Fraser River was too dangerous, a guide offered to direct them to the North Thompson River, which they could follow to Fort Kamloops and wait out the winter. But the Overlanders were anxious to get to the Cariboo. The Fraser River was fast-flowing and it was right in front of them. The men decided that most of them would build rafts and travel down the Fraser with McMicking. Another man, Archibald Thompson, volunteered to lead a second smaller group that would go with the Secwepemc guide and herd the animals along the North Thompson. Cardinal would stay with them as an interpreter.

Catherine was desperate to take the faster route so that she could get to a settlement before her baby came. But the men, who were unaware of her pregnancy since she kept it hidden beneath her long skirts, were concerned for her and the children. They insisted that the Schuberts go to the North Thompson with the guide.

When McMicking and his men left on their rafts, Catherine was sorry to see Dr. Stevenson leave. The next morning, September 2, she was among the group of thirty-six people who began a two-week ordeal of hacking their way through the woods. The Secwepemc guide ensured that Cardinal knew how to find the North Thompson, then he returned to Tête Jaune Cache. Cardinal stayed with them as long as he could, but once they made it to the river, he too needed to turn back if he had any hope of making it home to Fort Edmonton before winter.

Archibald Thompson and his group soon realized that it was impossible to walk along the banks of the North Thompson; the mountains came too close to the water. They would have to travel by raft. As there was no way to take the animals with them, the men killed the oxen and the Schuberts' old black cow. They smoked the meat, set the horses free and, in memoriam, blazed the words "Slaughter Camp" into a tree. Catherine wondered what she would do without milk for the children.

The group built rafts and canoes, and on the evening of September 21, they prepared for the next morning's start down the river. Catherine dressed the children in layers and packed their possessions into the large canoe Augustus had built. But overnight, the canoe washed away and Catherine woke to find that everything, including their food and the children's gifts she had bought, was gone. While Gus wailed about losing his buckskin suit, Catherine struggled to stay calm. Augustus hurried to build a raft, and the other men each approached Catherine, leaving with her a small portion of their rations before setting out ahead.

The Schubert family rafted down the North Thompson for three days before they saw two men returning with a warning. Downstream the river narrowed and passed between walls of jagged rock. It had hurled them over a 2-metre drop, and one of their rafts had overturned. Strachan, one of the men who had saved Kelso from drowning, had been killed.

Catherine and Augustus had no choice but to abandon their raft and set out on what turned into a three-day, 14-kilometre detour through the woods. They carried the children and what remained of their belongings until they came back to the river downstream of the rapids. Augustus built another raft, and again they set off on the North Thompson.

On October 7, more than two weeks after they had left "Slaughter Camp," the Schuberts were out of rations and ammunition for hunting. They came to a Secwepemc settlement that had been abandoned when many of the villagers had died of smallpox. Catherine and Augustus harvested the only food they could find. For the next four days on the raft, the family huddled under buffalo robes eating nothing but raw potatoes. When the potatoes ran out, the only food left for them to eat was some rose hips that Catherine managed to find on shore. Years later, in a letter to her granddaughter, Catherine would write, "I wondered how much longer we could all hang on, thinking that for sure I would lose my unborn child."

A week later Catherine was lying on the raft when she felt her first labour pains. It was October 13, 1862 — six weeks after the Schuberts had left Tête Jaune Cache — and a winter storm was developing. Although Fort Kamloops was within reach, Augustus feared that the baby would not wait. When a Secwepemc camp appeared on shore, he prayed that this one was inhabited.

Catherine sent Augustus to get help while she bundled her children in buffalo robes on the bank. At first the villagers regarded the frantic white man with suspicion, but upon following him to Catherine, one of the women understood. She ushered Catherine into a tent and retrieved her midwifery supplies. In the morning, Gus, Mary Jane and Jimmy had a new sister. Catherine told them, "I

named her Rose for the rose hips that saved our lives."

Later that day, the Schuberts continued to Fort Kamloops where they spent the winter. They learned that the men who had rafted down the Fraser River had completed their journey in just ten days as opposed to the six weeks it had taken the North Thompson group. They also heard about three other men who had drowned since leaving Tête Jaune Cache.

In the spring the family moved to Lillooet, 167 kilometres from Fort Kamloops. Although they would live there for most of the next fourteen years, Augustus spent long periods away in the Cariboo. He and Catherine had two more babies. She opened a hotel and taught local children in her home. She lobbied the government to build a school and was successful in 1873. Mary Jane, who was not yet sixteen, became the first teacher.

Four years later Catherine and the youngest children moved to Cache Creek, where she became both the matron and domestic science teacher at the boarding school. After Augustus retired from mining and they settled in Spallumcheen, British Columbia, Catherine convinced him to donate land for the first schoolhouse there, and she arranged to have an accredited teacher brought in.

Catherine raised six children and two of her grandchildren, and she improved access to education for many. She taught domestic skills to women who arrived with little concept of how to survive on the frontier. Skilled in midwifery and the use of medicinal herbs, Catherine was often called upon in times of need in the community. After her death in 1918, the people of Spallumcheen erected a monument bearing the words:

In honour of CATHERINE SCHUBERT
A brave and notable pioneer

How Do We Know
What We Know?

Catherine told the story of her journey to her family and friends. In 1915, three years before she died, she also wrote it down in a letter to one of her granddaughters. In the 1930s, more than seventy years after the expedition, Catherine's children Gus and Rose were both interviewed for local newspapers. At this time Jimmy also recorded everything his parents had told him about the trip. There is a copy of his "Reminiscences" available through the Archives of British Columbia.

During the trek, several of the Overlanders, including John Sellar, who travelled from Huntingdon, Quebec, and Thomas McMicking, kept journals. They rarely mention Catherine, but they do describe the events the Overlanders experienced.

What Do We Know?

Catherine was born in Ballybrick, Ireland. Her parents were James and Mary O'Hare and she was the youngest of nine children. When she emigrated to New York in 1850, she gave her age as sixteen, but baptism records suggest that she was probably born in 1837. She may have claimed to be older to hide that she was only thirteen and travelling alone.

The direction the Overlanders travelled is pretty clear thanks to Thomas McMicking's notes on the trek. They followed fur trade routes established by the Hudson Bay Company or paths known to their Indigenous guides.

Sketches and watercolours by William Hind, an artist who left Fort Garry a few days after the McMicking group, provide visual images of scenes and events along the journey.

What Don't We Know?

By the end of the journey, the Overlanders had a lot of respect for Catherine and appreciated her contributions to the trek. But some accounts claim that, at first, the men had a rule against women on the trail. Did Catherine have to argue or persuade them to let her go?

There isn't much recorded about the Métis, the Secwepemc or the other Indigenous people involved in the journey. McMicking wrote that he hired an Haudenosaunee guide in Fort Pitt who he called only "Mitchelle," which makes it difficult to learn any more about him. The official records state that seven people from the Red River settlement (or Fort Garry) joined the expedition. McMicking specifically mentions the Schubert family. But who were the two other people? One man wrote that they were French-speaking attendants of the Schuberts. Schubert family tradition seems to agree with this. In an interview many years later, Augustus Jr. (Gus) did say that a French Canadian voyageur helped his father build a canoe on the North Thompson River. Were the two other people in the records the family's Métis farmhands? Just as it's hard to discover more about Catherine, it's difficult to learn more about these other people who featured in the story when their names are absent from the pages.

A Sister Story

Charlotte Small

More than five decades before Catherine Schubert's expedition with the Overlanders, Charlotte Small crossed the Rocky Mountains with her children, Fanny, Samuel and Emma. Charlotte was a quiet woman from Île-à-la-Crosse, Saskatchewan. Her mother was Nehiyaw and her father a Scottish fur trader.

In 1799, at thirteen years old, Charlotte married the English mapmaker David Thompson and became essential to his exploration of much of the land west of the Great Lakes. In 1807 she helped to guide him and his party over the Rockies following a transportation route known to the area's Indigenous men and women for many years. When Charlotte returned across the mountains with her family a year later, she — like Catherine — was pregnant with her fourth baby. John was born two months later.

Charlotte's voice is faint — her story spoken, not recorded in the charts and records kept by the men, and only included sparsely in David Thompson's own journal — but she endured the same dangers, extremes of temperature, swamps and perilous river crossings as her husband.

Over thirteen years, Charlotte journeyed via canoe, horseback and foot across at least 20 000 kilometres. Yet to understand her story, we have to imagine much of it — like the terror she must have felt on the day David Thompson wrote, "One of my horses nearly crushing my children to death . . . I shot him on the spot and rescued my little ones." And we can only envision Charlotte's hours of agony when Emma, then two years old, disappeared along the edge of a river; the frantic search through bushes and logjams for her daughter's drowned body; and Charlotte's joy at nightfall when one of the men instead found her asleep on a snowbank.

Describing Charlotte in his journal, David called her his "great advantage." She knew how to survive on the prairie, how to prepare plants for food and medicine, and how to hunt and snare rabbits when meat was scarce. With her understanding of English, French and

Nehiyawewin, Charlotte was able to translate for him and to assist him in building relationships with people of different cultures. And she did all this while raising and caring for the five children they had over the years they were travelling.

In 1812 Charlotte and David moved to Terrebonne, Quebec, near Montreal. While many marriages between Indigenous women and European men dissolved when the men returned to the cities and towns, David and Charlotte reaffirmed their marriage in a church ceremony in Montreal. They eventually had thirteen children.

But life in the East was hard for Charlotte. Within a year of moving to Terrebonne, five-year-old John fell ill and died. Only a month later, David recorded in the family Bible that seven-year-old Emma was also "buried close touching her brother."

The Thompsons slipped into poverty as David slowly went blind. Charlotte and the children stayed with him in the East, many miles from her roots in Île-à-la-Crosse. In 1857, after a marriage of almost fifty-eight years, David passed away. Charlotte died only three months later. Charlotte and David were buried side-by-side in unmarked graves.

Seventy years following David Thompson's death, he was honoured as "the World's Greatest Geographer" by the Canadian Historical Association. In 1927 a monument was erected at his grave site and he was declared a Person of National Historic Significance. It would be

another eighty-seven years before Charlotte Small was
given her own memorial. In 2014 a plaque was unveiled
at the historic site of Rocky Mountain House in Alberta,
where Charlotte and David had sometimes wintered
as they explored the West. Her voice may be faint but
she is remembered as Charlotte Small, "Woman of the
Paddle Song."

The Secret Life of Miss Freeman

Alice Freeman

February 1888
Toronto, Ontario

Though the students at Ryerson School loved Miss Freeman, none of them knew her secret. At the end of the day, when they went home to their chores and their beds, she became Faith Fenton, investigative reporter for the *Empire* newspaper in Toronto, Ontario. She spent her nights doing things that surely no teacher would do — like interviewing famous actresses or visiting jails and homeless shelters, before walking home alone down dark city streets in the early hours of the morning. By the time her students arrived back at school, Miss Freeman was standing by her blackboard and the children had no idea where she had been only hours before.

Leading this kind of double life was not easy for a woman in the 1880s. No lady — and certainly no schoolteacher

— would look directly at a man and ask probing questions or dare to form her own opinion. This was a time of rigid rules and restrictions. Women were expected to behave modestly. At teacher-training school, female students were not even allowed to speak to the male students, and when they graduated they earned less than $300 a year — not even half of what a male teacher made.

If the Toronto school board were to hear that one of their women teachers had been walking the streets alone at night, she would be fired. But "Faith Fenton" was not one to keep quiet when she felt that women had no more freedom than five-year-old children, and Alice Freeman was used to doing things alone.

Growing up in a house full of children, Alice stood out in her family — the girl who was not "girly" or "pretty," the child with no musical talent, the one who was always off on her own thinking and writing.

When she was ten, her family moved from Bowmanville, Ontario to Barrie, Ontario. Then one day Alice's parents took her to Toronto, put her on a steamer, and shipped her back to Bowmanville to live with a childless couple, Reverend Reikie and his wife. Perhaps the Freemans felt that they were unable to provide for their many children — eventually there were twelve of them. Maybe Mrs. Freeman wanted to give Alice, her smart and literary daughter, access to the best education possible. Alice's older sister was already missing more and more school to stay home and help with the babies. Mrs. Reikie had the resources and the connections to offer Alice a formal education and to teach her the things she would need to know to succeed in society.

Still, Alice always remembered the day her parents left her at the Toronto pier — how she swallowed her fear as she walked onto the Royal Mail Line steamer, and how once her parents were out of sight, she lay down on a pile of life preservers and cried.

Now, on a cold day in February 1888, as Alice walked past dilapidated wood-framed cottages in Toronto's poorest quarter, her heart pounded. For two years she had been writing articles for the *Northern Advance*, a small paper in Barrie. But today she was looking for a story for her second column in the Toronto *Empire*, the newspaper founded by Sir John A. Macdonald himself.

Of course the respectable Miss Freeman of Ryerson could not be a newspaper reporter, exposed to details of heinous crimes, gritty political discussions and pressrooms full of men using foul language. So Alice had created "Faith Fenton," a pen name that was unapologetically female. "Faith" would become a voice for the country's impoverished people. She called them "the submerged tenth" of society as they were seemingly invisible, their concerns often overlooked or ignored by the more affluent.

Alice had heard that on Terauley Street there was a crèche, a place where mothers could leave their children while they went out to earn a few cents. In 1880s Toronto, it was believed that only the poorest, most unfortunate women would resort to such drastic measures, and many viewed the institutions that served them as disreputable. The plight of the poor needed attention and charity, but for the upper classes to respond, a call to action would have to be presented with the proper respectability.

At 260 Terauley, Alice found the matron sitting beside a cradle. As she stood up, the woman pried the fingers of a clinging four-year-old from her dress. She told the reporter that they often cared for between twenty and thirty children per week. Alice pulled out her writing pad and took notes. The crèche was open from 7 a.m. to 7 p.m.

and admitted children from infants to age seven.

From everything she had heard, Alice had her angle. She knew how to awaken the sympathies of her readers. She would describe her visit in sweeping detail, her style like that of Charles Dickens, a writer whom Victorian readers loved. Alice chose her words carefully. Begging was too crass to appeal to the upper crust of Toronto society. Instead she offered her readers a sense of the warmth that would come from their generosity. She wrote that she had reassured the matron that the people of Toronto were loving enough "to fill these small rooms to overflowing with all that is necessary."

Within the week, Alice saw readers responding. She was inspired to devote future columns to orphanages, homes for elderly women and Toronto's Hospital for Sick Children. Two weeks after Alice's visit to a homeless women's shelter, she received a letter of thanks saying that the shelter had received donations of money and food, and even the offer of medical care from one of the city's doctors. Alice's column, intended to serve as a part of the paper's "Woman's Pages," was eliciting a response from both men and women.

Alice dedicated articles to issues of child abuse and the wage gap between male and female employees. She addressed discrimination against women that ranged from unfair hiring practices to the lack of public women's restrooms, which made it difficult for a woman to go far from her home, especially with her children. She was disgusted by sexual harassment on Toronto streets, particularly when it was perpetrated by well-dressed, middle-aged men whom she called "vultures."

As reporter Faith Fenton's reputation grew so did Alice's access to politicians, entertainers and great speakers. She met Susan B. Anthony, leader of the American women's suffrage movement, which eventually won the right for women to vote; Emily Stowe, the first practising female doctor in Canada; and Lady Aberdeen, the founder and president of the National Council of Women of Canada (NCWC). To many, those who argued for women's equality were considered pushy and shrill — and therefore unwomanly — which alienated some women who might otherwise be supporters. So Alice cloaked her arguments in language that allowed her readers to sympathize while retaining their own womanliness and respectability.

While Alice advocated for the rights of all women during her years at the Toronto *Empire*, she remained particularly concerned about poor women, who were doubly downtrodden, since there were few respectable ways for women to make money.

In January 1895, Alice decided to investigate the House of Industry, a place where women could work in exchange for a meal and a bed. But by then "Faith Fenton" had

already visited — and exposed — many of the less repu-
table institutions in the city. She could not just show up
at the door. She needed a disguise.

One night, shivering in a patched overcoat, an old
sweater and a frayed black skirt, she pushed open the
door to that sombre building and identified herself as
Mary Smith from Hamilton. The two men in the office did
not look happy.

"Hamilton should look after its own poor," one
grumbled.

He led her to the elderly caretaker, Mrs. Goberly, who
muttered that it was past nine o'clock and the shelter was
closed. She ushered Alice into a lavatory.

"Get yer things off, an' take yer bath," Mrs. Goberly
commanded, arms crossed and watching her.

Alice was shocked. When she had toured the Jarvis
Street Mission, she had been told that the men were only
forced to bathe if they were especially dirty.

"But I don't need a bath," pleaded Alice.

Mrs. Goberly would not be moved. "Need it or not,
you've got to have it!"

She stood on guard while Alice removed her clothes
and supervised while she took her bath.

Suffering from a cold, Alice was chilled and coughing
by the time she stepped out of the water. When the caretaker handed her a nightdress, she took pity and gave

back Alice's sweater and stockings too. Mrs. Goberly led Alice upstairs to the women's sleeping quarters. As she opened the door, a wave of hot, fetid air rushed out. Alice thought about leaving while she could, but if she walked out now she would never get the full story.

Six women were resting on camp beds and Alice took the seventh. It was wrapped in a dark blanket with a straw pillow at the head. Mrs. Goberly handed her two covers she swore were "never used afore" and then she left, shutting the door behind her. Alice lay in darkness, listening to a woman sobbing. Others were restless, tossing and muttering. In her head, the reporter began composing her story, referring to herself as "the woman." Her description of what happened to her next was horrifying:

The woman . . . tossed uneasily; little nips and prickles beset her arms and neck. Suddenly, with a vague fear, she turned to look closely at her pillow — then her heart sank . . . Bugs! . . . Great, plump, sluggish creatures — a dozen she counted, moving steadily down her pillow. How many more the dark blankets held she could not tell . . .

Alice jumped up to cover the mattress with the blankets the caretaker had given her, but the heated room had grown so thick with the women's breath — never mind the

smell of whiskey from one of the women in the corner —
that she thought she would open the door.

"What be's yer doin'?" called a voice.

Alice explained that she could not tolerate the heat
any more. The voice responded that it was better than
opening the door to the rats in the corridor. "It's real bold
they are!"

The reporter lay in the dark, watching the room grow
faintly lighter until morning broke and the other women
began to rise. She ran down to the lavatory, dressed, and
rushed to the outside door.

"Where are you goin'?" came a voice from behind her.

Alice explained that she had to leave, although she did
not say that she was desperate to go home to have a bath
and to put the night behind her. The caretaker pushed her
out of the way and locked the door. She slipped the key
into her pocket and said, "Not . . . until you've done a bit
of scrubbin' or washin' to pay yer night's lodgin'."

Alice begged to do her chores quickly, saying that
she had a job to get to. But seven o'clock turned into
eight o'clock and then nine o'clock, and still the door was
locked. It was 10 a.m. before the "laundry missis" arrived
to assign the women their duties. At this point, Alice simply refused to work. She was told that she could leave but
she would never be able to spend another night at the
House of Industry. She was not upset.

Two weeks after printing Alice's exposé, the *Empire* was taken over by another newspaper. All its columnists were let go and Alice Freeman, who had only recently quit her job of nineteen years as a school teacher, was unemployed. However, Faith Fenton now had a name in the newspaper world. Before the end of the year, Alice would become Canada's first woman editor at the *Canadian Home Journal*. In this position, she became even more outspoken and demonstrated greater public support to Lady Aberdeen's NCWC. Because of this, she was fired from the paper. This was at the same time as she was named "the head of the lady journalists in Toronto."

While being unemployed could have been catastrophic for a forty-year-old single woman, Alice had her connections. In April 1898, four members of the Victorian Order of Nurses — also founded by Lady Aberdeen — were leaving to accompany the two-hundred-man Yukon Field Force heading to the Klondike goldfields to maintain law and order. Alice arranged to join them as a correspondent for Toronto's *Globe* newspaper.

She and the nurses took a train to Vancouver, British Columbia, where the soldiers of the Yukon Field Force joined them. On May 15 they all boarded a steamer north to Wrangell, Alaska, where they transferred to riverboats, which would take them up the Stikine River to Glenora. There the real challenge began: a 250-kilometre

march north to Teslin Lake, on the border between British Columbia and Yukon. The trail took them through mountain passes, along treacherous rocky ledges and over gnarled roots and fallen trees. They slogged through bogs in which their mules sank up to their bellies and the women's skirts turned to lead weights. They suffered relentless mosquitoes and trudged through endless forests, which were sometimes smouldering from fires caused by the six thousand prospectors who had cooked and lived along the trail in 1898.

This was the Stikine route to the Klondike — a trek known to turn away or kill more than half of those who took it and one of the hardest journeys ever made by Canadian troops. At some point, Alice fell ill — a fact that she never reported in her columns. Reverend John Pringle, a Presbyterian minister working in Yukon, found her sick in an overcrowded tent with the other women. He took pity and gave her a tent of her own.

At Teslin Lake, Alice's party built boats and travelled via river and lake to Fort Selkirk, Yukon, where the soldiers would remain. The entire journey from Wrangell to Fort Selkirk had taken four months, but still Alice had not yet reached her destination. There was a steamer for Dawson leaving an hour after they arrived and Alice boarded it. By the end of September, she was camped out in her little tent pitched on the site of the barracks of the North West Mounted Police.

In Dawson Alice felt utterly alone. The nurses were out in the tent cities, battling a typhoid epidemic, and she was sick and cold with nothing but a canvas roof over her head. With the rivers beginning to freeze, there was little chance of returning to Toronto before spring. Alice wondered if she would have to take up cooking or washing in order to make a living.

Fortunately her reputation attracted the attention of Dr. John Brown, who was both the doctor and Territorial Secretary to William Ogilvie, Commissioner of Yukon. She soon became Ogilvie's assistant private secretary. Alice continued writing about two columns a month for the *Globe* and she staked her own gold claims that were eventually valued at $2000. On January 1, 1900, she married John Brown. Alice had often advised her women readers not to choose marriage over work simply because it was expected of them. When she left her independent lifestyle, it was "to become the wife of the man she loved."

Alice and John lived in Yukon for four more years. In 1905 they moved to Toronto, where John had accepted a position at Toronto General Hospital. They travelled extensively together. While they never had children, they doted on their nieces and nephews, often taking Alice's niece, Olive, on their travels. Alice enjoyed these years and wrote only when she felt compelled to do so.

Alice's seventy-ninth birthday would have been January 14, 1936. Instead this was the day of her funeral. She was buried in Toronto's Mount Pleasant Cemetery with a headstone bearing both the names Alice Freeman and Faith Fenton.

How Do We Know What We Know?

Alice Freeman as Faith Fenton wrote for several newspapers, expressing her thoughts and ideas publicly for over forty years. Articles she wrote for the Toronto *Empire* provide much insight into the Faith Fenton side of the woman. The details about Alice Freeman's life are much harder to discover.

With access to Alice's family archives and memorabilia for her research, Jill Downie wrote a biography called *A Passionate Pen: The Life and Times of Faith Fenton.* Through this book, along with "Faith's" articles, we can start to piece together Alice Freeman's story.

What Do We Know?

From her columns, we know that Alice was not afraid to express her opinions, that she was angered by issues of discrimination or unfairness, and that she was a strong supporter of equality for women in all areas.

Although Alice always wrote under a woman's name, Faith Fenton was not the first pen name she used. From 1886 to 1888, she wrote for the *Northern Advance* in Barrie, Ontario, signing her name as Stella. When she changed her pen name to Faith, she chose the title of a poem she liked as inspiration. In it, the subject keeps her lamp burning through adversity and becomes a torch of hope from which others can take a spark. Fenton was her grandfather's surname at birth. He lived in England where he ran away to London with an actress, became a writer, and changed his name to Freeman.

What Don't We Know?

We don't know who knew about Alice/Faith's double identity. She lived with her younger brother Fred and his wife, and the rest of her family knew as well. As a woman, Alice needed an escort when she went on assignment. Was this person always a family member or one of the men from the newspaper? Did she ever have to tell her friends or anyone else? Did no one at her school ever suspect?

Perhaps a better question to ask about Alice Freeman is *why* don't we know the answers to these questions. How did the story of a famous Canadian journalist somehow become not-so-famous?

Was it hidden in the events after Alice's death? Her husband John, then seventy-four years old, married Alice's niece, Olive, who was forty-five. In the family's efforts to put the scandal behind them, Alice's story — and the legacy of Faith Fenton — was forgotten.

Or was Alice silenced because she was too outspoken, offending some of the men in her profession and calling into question long-standing policies and prejudices that hurt women and children?

A Sister Story

Lucile Hunter

In 1897, a year before Alice Freeman made her well-documented trek to Yukon, Lucile Hunter was there. Her story, however, is harder to find. Eighteen and pregnant, Lucile hauled her gear up the punishing Stikine Trail alongside her husband, Charles, before the main hordes of prospectors flooded into Dawson in 1898, before the Yukon Field Force and Victorian Order of Nurses were there for support and before all the good claims were staked.

In her later years, Lucile loved to entertain visitors. Perhaps if we could have visited her in her small cabin in Whitehorse, she would have told us the story herself of how she was one of the first Black people to join the Klondike Gold Rush. We could have asked her where she was when gold fever spread through North America. Did she and Charles make their way to Seattle, Washington, to board a steamer up the coast, or were they already there? Since we cannot ask Lucile for her story, we must instead try to piece it together through the recollections of those who remember her.

Having taken a steamer up to Wrangell, Alaska, she and Charles would have boarded a riverboat that would take them along the Stikine River to Glenora in the Interior of British Columbia. From there, they would have begun the 250-kilometre trek on foot north to Teslin Lake, which spans the border between B.C. and Yukon.

Over half of the seven thousand people who attempted this trail did not make it. Like them, Lucile would have faced the most extreme weather, swarms of biting insects and forbidding terrain as she clambered over jagged rocks and fallen trees. Did she tie up her skirt or attempt to shorten it like Alice Freeman did? How exhausted did she grow, carrying up to 34 kilograms of mining tools, camping equipment and utensils, along with the growing child in her belly? And still, each night, she would have cooked dinner for herself and Charles and prepared the next day's food.

Years later Lucile told a reporter that, despite all the trek's challenges, she never became disheartened;

traversing the Stikine Trail was simply one of the events of her life. Lucile was strong, resilient, no fuss. She was the woman who arrived ready to give birth in -52°C on the south shore of Teslin Lake where there was only one cabin. In that cabin by herself, she delivered Marie Elizabeth, or "Teslin."

Most of the other prospectors waited out the winter along the frozen lakes and rivers. They would continue their journey to the Klondike by boat after the ice broke in the spring. But old friends say that Lucile and Charles found a dog team and pressed on alone. They would have mushed hundreds of kilometres over land and ice. Lucile carried newborn Teslin, their faces wrapped to protect their eyes from snow blindness and their lungs from the -50°C temperatures.

It is possible that the Hunters passed others escaping starvation in Dawson along the way. By the time they arrived, food stocks were so low that every restaurant had closed, and even people being arrested had to bring their own food to jail. Perhaps this is why Lucile and Charles moved on to Bonanza Creek. They staked their first claim on February 26, 1898, beating out all those who would arrive in the spring to find most of the claims already taken.

And then came the mining. Some say Lucile worked alongside her husband as he dug for gold. Did she lower herself down — 12 to 18 metres below the surface of the earth — and squeeze herself into tunnels to carve and hack her way through the frozen dirt?

Lucile handled the business and the paperwork; she raised their daughter; and she opened a roadhouse — a refuge for miners far from home — that offered bannock, bacon or beans and a friendly smile. It likely had a dirt floor, a low roof and no windows. What little light it had would have been provided by candles. Lucile's work would have been hard and exhausting with the food kept in an animal-proof box, a woodstove that needed constant attention and ice that had to be thawed before cooking or washing.

When Teslin was eleven, she was sent to school in Seattle, Washington. Not long after, Lucile and Charles staked silver claims in Mayo, Yukon — 225 kilometres from Dawson. For decades Lucile monitored the mines in both places. With no car, how many kilometres did she travel as she walked back and forth each year?

Lucile and Charles visited Teslin in Seattle, where she married her husband, Carl Sorensen. Teslin died at twenty-seven, and they brought her five-year-old son, Carl Leo or "Buster," to Dawson where they raised him as their own. He called Lucile "Mom."

After Charles died in 1939, Buster moved with Lucile to Whitehorse, Yukon. Although at first she only had a tent, Lucile set up a laundry to wash the clothes of the Alaska Highway builders — those battalions of soldiers, many of them Black, that were sent in to build a 2400-kilometre road in eight months. Buster eventually moved out and he was stationed in Europe during World War II. Even though Lucile was then alone and her eyesight began to fail, she continued running the laundry and returning to Dawson to monitor her claims. For years after Charles died, she was the only known Black person in Yukon.

Lucile's great granddaughter Carol remembers her as Nana Hunter, a tall, strong-looking lady who wore her long grey-white hair braided and pinned up. She says Lucile secretly slipped the children cookies and cinnamon hearts when their mother was not looking.

By the 1950s Lucile could barely see, and the community pitched in to help her out. Neighbours cut wood or helped with the groceries. John Firth, a young boy at the time, remembers delivering baskets of food to her kitchen with its "airtight wood stove, one chair covered by a blanket, painted gold pans, and wooden crates that filled the rest of the space from floor to ceiling. A lifetime crammed into one room and illuminated by dim light barely filtering through the single, unwashed windowpane in front of her house."

And then the accumulated possessions of that lifetime were consumed by fire on December 6, 1961, when Lucile's cabin burned down. The fear she must have felt, sensing the light from the flames, hearing the crackle and smelling the smoke, as she groped for the door and the knife she kept through the latch as a bolt. A neighbour rescued her, but not before the fringes of Lucile's clothing caught fire.

Her home was destroyed. Friends offered Lucile a basement apartment downtown and helped her to continue living alone. When she later moved to the Whitehorse General Hospital, they visited her there. It was at Whitehorse General that the ceremony was held to bestow upon Lucile Hunter honorary membership in the Yukon Order of Pioneers for her perseverance as a miner. She was their first female member.

Lucile died on June 10, 1972, at ninety-three years old, and we will never hear the story in her own voice. But thanks to John Firth, we can picture her in her little cabin as she bid visitors goodbye "always with the hint of a crooked smile . . . [as] she leaned forward onto her cane, chuckled and tilted her head as if sharing an intimate joke with her right shoulder."

Standing Her Ground

Cougar Annie

1920s
Boat Basin, Vancouver Island, British Columbia

Survival at Boat Basin was a struggle for Ada Annie Rae-Arthur and her husband, Willie. There were weeks when porridge was all that they and their children had to eat, so Ada's goats were the most valuable thing on their land. Ada had built pens to protect her animals, but still the cougars were drawn to their scent. There were times that the big cats took a goat, sometimes more than one. If the cougars killed all of them, there would be no milk for anyone.

Ada had been a sharpshooter since she was eight years old in South Africa — and she always protected what was hers. One night she said to Willie, "If those goats are like cougar bait, then that's how we'll use 'em."

She picked out a goat, tethered it to a stake and left it in the dark until she heard its terrified bleating. Then Ada returned, her gun on one shoulder and a lantern raised above her head. The goat was wild with fear. There was surely a cougar out there somewhere.

Ada scanned the darkness. By the wheelbarrow, two large, yellow eyes glowed back at her. Although in the cedar forests of Vancouver Island Ada was hunting a cougar instead of a lion, her approach stayed the same as when she was a girl in South Africa. She had to sight fast and shoot for the heart if she wanted to ensure a kill. Without lowering the lantern, Ada aimed and fired. A thud. One less predator to steal her precious goats.

Ada enjoyed the company of animals more than she did that of people. As a child, she was not allowed around other children much, and she got most of her education at home. Her father, George Jordan, had dragged Ada and her mother with him as he moved from California to England, New Zealand, Australia, South Africa and Canada. When Ada got older and met a young man, her father refused to let her have a relationship with him. Somehow Willie Rae-Arthur was different. There was something about him that made even George Jordan let him stick around.

But by 1915, when Ada and Willie had been married and living in Vancouver, British Columbia, for six years, Willie had spent most of their money on drugs and alcohol. George realized that Willie needed to get out of Vancouver, away from temptation. With the help of Willie's sister in Scotland, he arranged for Ada, Willie and their children to move to the west coast of Vancouver Island.

There in the harbour, Ada Annie, who was five months pregnant, hauled herself off a steamer and into a dugout canoe. She and Willie loaded up four-year-old George, three-year-old Frank, one-year-old Margaret, their cow and whatever household goods Willie had not sold off.

Out where few newcomers wanted to settle, the government offered pre-emption land, which gave settlers permission to live on uncleared acres as long as they developed them and proved that they were able to grow crops there. Willie's 117 acres were set back from the beach in the rainforest. On the land was a small wooden cabin. As her family trudged through the woods, Ada kept her shotgun under her arm. There were cougars and bears out there — and she would kill anything that got too close.

The baby was born just months after they arrived. When the pains started, Ada collected the things she needed for birthing a baby. Father Moser, the priest from a nearby Roman Catholic mission, arrived with a Hesquiaht midwife, but Ada told them to wait the night out in an old shack down by the beach. Willie could get them if there was a problem — although Ada knew she would have to find Willie first. By then he would be somewhere passed out drunk.

Three days after Isobel was born, Ada was back working the land. She left her youngest children in the cabin with the cookstove burning low. Margaret and Frank were in the pen Ada had built for them, and baby Isobel was in her bed. George would be five in a couple of weeks, and he could be helpful to her outside. Ada was clearing the trees on their land in order to plant potatoes and other vegetables.

Willie was very little help. He was useless with tools and got lost if he so much as stepped off the trail. It was easier if Ada expected nothing of him. He would watch the babies sometimes — draw pictures, sing songs or make up stories for them. At least that was something.

Ada worked sixteen-hour days or longer. As the children grew, they helped her to chop wood, plant vegetables, fetch water and feed animals. She burned out the stumps of the huge trees that they felled and somehow Ada cleared five farmable acres.

After Isobel, baby Rose came along and then Helen. The family of eight lived in that single-room cabin. They collected water in rain barrels or pulled it out of the nearby creek. While the kids played with the Hesquiaht children, Ada preferred to keep to herself.

By 1923, eight years after arriving at Boat Basin, Ada had managed to put in an acre of potatoes and another of vegetables. She had a couple of acres of grass, one hundred chickens, four black pigs, and a shed for her goats. To make money, she raised minks, rabbits and guinea pigs to be slaughtered for their meat and fur. Ada also hunted and trapped, then sold pelts and collected a bounty on the cougars she killed. But she needed a more reliable way of making money.

Ada started experimenting with shrubs, trees and plants. She had learned more than just shooting in South Africa — she even won a horticulture competition when she was fourteen. Now she was looking to the future. She had proven that she could grow crops on their acres, and

it seemed the government was going to officially grant Willie the land. With the boys' help, he had started building a four-room house with proper milled lumber. She had a family with six strong, healthy children — four of them big enough to work — and another baby on the way. Ada was going to launch a horticultural business, a plant nursery that would ship rare bulbs all over the world.

But then the land examiner reported that Ada and Willie's children were being neglected. The Children's Aid Society took George, Frank, Margaret and Isobel away to Vancouver, where they would go to school. Without her children, aged eight to thirteen, Ada was left with the new baby Tommy and only the two youngest girls to help — all while she was trying to get her business off the ground.

With the extra work that she now had to do all on her

own, Ada would not leave Boat Basin, not even to visit her children in Vancouver. For the next three years, she struggled, never laying eyes on them.

In 1926 another baby was born, but Agnes lived only forty-five minutes. Ada buried her in the garden out by the back gate. She wondered how her plans for the future had turned into such a mess. She decided to write to the children's school in Vancouver to tell them she and Willie were perfectly capable of providing for their family. Still the children were kept away. George and Frank were almost full-grown men before they were allowed to go home, and Margaret and Isobel were teenagers. Another baby, Lawrence or "Laurie," had been born by that time.

With all eight children now at home, Ada opened a store in her front room where she sold provisions, including her own chicken eggs, to customers around the harbour or workers passing through. She trapped and shot cougars, referring to her hunting grounds as Cougar Alley. Years later Ada would tell a reporter that she had killed sixty-two cougars and eighty black bears — and that she had collected bounty on ten of them in one year. People began calling her Cougar Annie.

By 1936 two more baby girls had been born. Neither of them lived very long, and Ada buried them beside Agnes. Ada and Willie's older children were now grown, and only Helen, Tommy and Laurie still lived at home.

It was the children who came across their father's boat on the shore one day with no sign of Willie anywhere. Ada stayed out all that night searching, but morning came and she still had not found him. Later that day his body washed up. Ada buried it in her garden, heaping stones on his grave to keep animals from digging him up.

She was a woman alone on her land. Still Ada intended to stay. She was finally making money and her nursery was growing. It was famous for having some of the best vegetables and flowers and more than 200 varieties of dahlias. She brought in plants from places as far away as Japan, Chile and New Zealand. She needed help.

So she ran an ad for a new husband in a Saskatchewan newspaper saying she was a B.C. widow and nursery owner in need of a partner — preferably one who was also looking for marriage. Several men tried to fill the position. None of them turned out to be a particularly good fit.

There were stories that Ada's second husband, George Campbell, threatened to kill her if she did not give him money. The medical report after his death stated that the gun hanging on the wall was accidentally discharged into his thigh. Ada had several explanations for how this might have happened.

Ada's third husband, Esau Arnold, was a good worker, but unfortunately he had an accident chopping wood or felling a tree and he died in the hospital not long after.

One rumour had it that her fourth husband, George Lawson, tried to throw Ada off a cliff. She told everyone that she ran him off with a shotgun. When he died years later, she did not marry again.

In 1967 Robert Culver, who had lived with Ada briefly in 1955, returned to Boat Basin. The cabin still had an outhouse, a wood fire for cooking, rain barrels for drinking water and no electricity. Ada was in her eighties and going blind. Robert was half-deaf. After five years at Boat Basin, he decided to leave. He begged Ada to go with him, but she insisted on remaining near her garden.

In 1983, ninety-five-year-old Ada was taken from her home and placed into hospital. Those who visited said that her thoughts were so much back in Boat Basin that she never truly left. Before she died in 1985, she arranged for her ashes to be scattered in her garden back by the orchard, close to Willie and her three babies.

Cougar Annie's garden serves as her memorial. To this day, she has stayed put.

How Do We Know What We Know?

In 1936 Ada convinced the government that Boat Basin had a large enough population to need its own post office, and that she should be its postmistress. For almost fifty years, she ran the post office out of her store — a very helpful arrangement for her mail-order nursery. As the postmistress she was responsible for updating the British Columbia directories that recorded the town's population. She often inflated the population by listing herself multiple times. Even so, we rely on post office documents for pieces of Ada's story.

As Ada's health failed later in life, a good friend, Peter Buckland, sent people to her cabin to take care of her. Her story comes to us through them and through Peter. Much of it is recorded in a book by Margaret Horsfield called *Cougar Annie's Garden.*

What Do We Know?

Ada liked to wear gumboots, a straw hat and a brown woollen cardigan over the same long dress that she wore for fifty years. She had bright blue eyes and would eat ice cream every day if she could. Animals loved her and she was particularly fond of her goats. If a goat went missing, one of the children would be sent out after it — even if it took the child all night to find the animal.

She was not the only cougar hunter on Vancouver Island, but most of the others hunted with dogs. Ada, instead, often caught cougars in traps.

What Don't We Know?

Cougar Annie was named Ada Annie Jordan at birth, but then through marriage she changed her last name to Rae-Arthur, Campbell, Arnold and Lawson. Regardless, she signed her business letters with her initials A.A. No one ever seemed to know what to call her. Many of her business contacts addressed her as Mr. — and that suited Ada fine. Her father, Willie and Robert Culver all called her Ada, but toward the end of her life, many others called her Granny.

Because Ada kept herself removed from most people — including those who lived in the Hesquaiht village not even 10 kilometres across the harbour — there aren't many people who can tell us about her. Most of her husbands didn't last long, and her daughters left home in their teens. Ada outlived all of her sons but one. Only Tommy was with her at the end of her life. The stories told by her caretakers and Peter Buckland only tell us what Ada wanted us to know — and she believed more in the art of crafting a good story than in always relating the facts.

Under a Cloak of Secrecy

Victoria Cheung

December 1925
Kongmoon (present-day Jiangmen), China

Returning to the Marion Barclay Hospital at the South China Mission in 1925, Dr. Victoria Cheung was shocked to find it a scene of devastation. Missionaries in Kongmoon (present-day Jiangmen) had found themselves in the middle of tensions that would eventually lead to the Chinese Civil War. Their mission, which included the women's hospital that Victoria was in charge of, had been closed for months. During the missionaries' absence, looters had stolen all of the medical equipment.

Victoria did not know how long it might take to repair the damage to the building, but she did know that a hospital was more than walls and beds. It was doctors, nurses, staff and patients — patients who came for surgery; for treatment of diseases like dysentery, tuberculosis or cholera; for vaccinations; or for a safe place to deliver their babies. And Victoria was skilled at providing all of this care.

Having been in Kongmoon for more than two years, she was used to working with limited access to medical supplies and without running water and electricity. So with her team of local staff and Canadian missionaries, Victoria set up an outside care centre near the building site. She would supervise construction while continuing to provide medical treatment for patients. Fortunately the rebuilding was complete within three months — before the coming typhoon season.

As a child in Canada, Victoria had always known she wanted to work in Kwangtung province (present-day Guangdong) where her parents had lived before they emigrated. It was there, in that place with a desperate need for doctors, especially for women and children, that Victoria's mother, Pat Ka, had received her own medical training. After she had moved to Victoria, British Columbia, to join her husband, Sing Noon, and even after having her first baby, Pat Ka continued to work as a midwife. When Victoria was three years old, her mother placed her in the Chinese Girls' Rescue Home so that Victoria would be well taken care of while her mother was out tending to others.

Victoria, also determined to study women's medicine, graduated from high school in 1916. But racism at that time made it almost impossible for a person of

Chinese heritage to become a doctor in British Columbia, and there were few Canadian medical schools that would admit women. So when the Presbyterian Woman's Missionary Society offered Victoria a scholarship to the University of Toronto's medical school, she headed east — leaving behind her parents, her younger brothers Herbert and Wilson, her eleven-year-old sister Alice and the city for which Victoria was named. She would become one of the first people of Asian heritage to graduate from the University of Toronto's medical school and the first woman intern at Toronto General Hospital.

Finally, in 1923, Victoria was able to fulfill her dream of travelling to Kwangtung as a medical missionary. Her brother Herbert had already moved to Chicago and Alice had died the year before, but Wilson and their parents followed Victoria to Kongmoon, Kwangtung.

For the rest of Victoria's life, she served the people in South China, working closely with her mother. Together they fostered a strong network of skilled women that would come to include Victoria's cousin Mei Siu, who was a nurse; Dr. Annie Wong; and another nurse, Lo Sui Chan. Over the decades, the women persevered through wars, epidemics and disasters, even if that meant working from secret clinics, putting themselves in great danger to do so.

In 1937, as World War II loomed, Victoria took a church-mandated break from missionary work. She used the opportunity to visit Toronto before heading to London, England, to further her studies at the School of Tropical Medicine.

That July, Japanese troops invaded China, sparking a war between the two nations. Victoria was anxious for the hospital, its patients and her staff back in China, so she booked her return passage for early 1938.

When she arrived in Kongmoon, Victoria found the compound vibrating with nervous tension. Bombers droned overhead, sometimes several times daily. The mission staff had been asked by Japanese troops to paint British flags on the roofs of all their buildings, including the new kindergarten, as foreign structures were not targets for Japanese attacks.

The mission's boarding school students had built their own bomb shelter. They had picked a room downstairs in the middle of the school and enlisted their teachers' help to pile sandbags all around it. Every night air raid sirens filled the air, a runner rushed along the bank of the river banging a gong and the school bell rang, signalling everyone to get to a shelter. The noise of the alarms was often drowned out by deafening explosions as bombs hit their mark. About 90 kilometres from Kongmoon, Canton (present-day Guangzhou) was under heavy attack.

After Canton was captured by Japanese troops, people from surrounding villages began to flee to the port in

Kongmoon. Victoria's colleagues prepared large amounts of soup that they carried out to the wharf while Victoria assessed the refugees there. She arranged for those who needed medical care to be sent to her hospital, and to others, she offered shelter in the mission's school. The South China Mission compound became a temporary refugee camp.

Then, on March 28, 1939, Kongmoon port was attacked as well. Victoria, who was in Hong Kong at the time, returned to find that the windows in her house had been shattered. One of the hospital workers had been injured, and a servant had been killed when a bomb hit the compound, bursting right through the British flag painted on the roof of the nurses' residence. When nearby villages were attacked too, Victoria and the other missionaries went out and carried injured people back to the hospital. Eventually they sheltered two hundred of the most desperate people — most of them women and children.

Even with the four or five missionaries stationed in Kongmoon, it was a struggle to provide care for the ninety children, some of whom were orphans and many others who were young girls with nowhere to go. They had been left at the hospital gate by mothers who knew it was their daughters' only chance for survival. But it would only get harder for Victoria to care for all these "foster children." Soon her staff was greatly reduced.

Japanese soldiers arrived and demanded that all women missionaries leave China. Victoria had no intention of going. She knew how much she was needed by her patients, the orphans and her team. Additionally, just before she and her parents had left for China, Canada had enacted the Chinese Exclusion Act, which prevented Chinese people from immigrating to Canada. There would be no exceptions, even though Pat Ka had already lived in Canada for years. And Victoria would not leave China if her mother was unable to return to British Columbia with her. Determined to remain in Kongmoon, Victoria hid her passport and hoped no one would divulge that she was Canadian. They did not.

With the other women missionaries evacuated, Victoria was left in charge of the men's and women's hospitals, the refugee camp and all correspondence back to the Woman's Missionary Society in Canada. Often she sat down at her typewriter and struggled to think of what to write. Her

first reports included statements about how she was anxious for the Canadian women to return. Victoria described the difficulty of providing food for all the orphans at the refugee camp, and a region so desperate that two children had been trampled to death in a stampede at a rice line. But as the mission's orphans grew stronger, Victoria's reports grew more optimistic.

Then, on December 8, 1941, Japanese soldiers marched into the compound and demanded the keys. They stationed a guard at the gates and refused to let anybody — including the students — go home. Victoria was ordered to hand over the hospital as the soldiers began removing equipment and all supplies of wheat, rice and medicine. She knew to co-operate with the guards.

Later that same afternoon, two officers arrived and gave the order that the students could be released. But forty-seven children, ranging from babies to sixteen-year-olds, had nowhere to go. They stayed with Victoria, along with twelve of her patients. A week later, all the male missionaries and other foreign men in China were evacuated. As Victoria watched a military truck drive away with her friends and colleagues, she felt a brief moment of hopelessness. But her thoughts soon turned to the orphans and patients she had to care for.

Unfortunately the Japanese soldiers had other plans for the hospital, and they took over the compound as a military base. Victoria, her team and the school's teachers were commanded to pack what was left of their belongings and leave. Having earned the friendship of many people in the area, the women rented two houses in Kongmoon port where they set up a small school and Victoria established a clinic. Using secret messages, she told the church not to contact her anymore.

Over the next four years, Victoria, her mother, Dr. Wong and the nurses secretly provided medical care to the people of Kongmoon. They set up three more clinics in the countryside and walked the many dangerous kilometres between them until Japan surrendered in 1945.

In October, as soon as the soldiers were driven from the compound, Victoria sent for the other missionaries to return. Concerned about her, the Church immediately began planning to send her on leave. But Victoria did not return to Canada until almost two years later; there was too much damage to the compound and too much work to be done. Everything, even utensils and wooden ceilings, had been taken from the buildings, and there were no linens in the hospital except for three mouldy sheets.

The peace that followed felt like a blessing but it was short-lived. The Communist party, suspicious of non-Chinese organizations in China, was gaining strength in its struggle to control the country. The missionaries were interrogated and some were arrested. Others were sent home. Eventually all foreign missions were shut down for good. Still Victoria Cheung stayed in Kongmoon.

From 1950 on the Church received very little news about Victoria. She was recognized by the Chinese government as a "national hero of culture," she adopted a son, and she continued to provide medical treatment to patients in the countryside around Kongmoon. Her mother worked with her until she passed away in 1965. In 1966 the Woman's Missionary Society received word that Victoria herself had died of cancer.

At her funeral in China, thousands lined the route and three thousand wreaths were laid on her casket. On December 8, 2012, Victoria, British Columbia, celebrated "Dr. Victoria Chung Day." All of this recognition Victoria herself would have completely dismissed. As she once told the *Toronto Star* upon turning them down for an interview, "There isn't anything to say about me."

How Do We Know
What We Know?

Victoria wrote many reports and letters during the time that she was Corresponding Secretary for the South China Mission. As the Chief Administrator for the Marion Barclay Hospital, she often filed the annual report. Many of these original documents are in The United Church of Canada Archives in Toronto. The archives also has a pamphlet prepared by the Woman's Missionary Society in 1945 that features her story.

Several newspaper articles were written about Victoria – some when she was in Canada on leave and some written more recently by Dr. John Price, a historian at the University of Victoria. Dr. Price and his colleague Ningping Yu have interviewed some of the family and friends who knew Victoria in Kongmoon, collecting stories and information for a biography about her life.

What Do We Know?

Victoria's school and university records tell us a lot about her early life. During her time at Victoria High School, she strived for perfect attendance and she had a good friend named Evylin Lucas. Together they were part of the school's Scottish Dance group. Victoria got A's in geometry and algebra, so she helped Evylin, who in turn assisted Victoria with her essays.

Victoria and her parents had both Chinese names and English names, and Chinese names written in the English alphabet can end up with several different spellings. In Canada Victoria

sometimes listed her name as Toy Mea or Choy Mei. Her last name was often spelled Chung. However, in the letters available at The United Church of Canada Archives, Victoria always spelled her name Cheung. In China she was known as Zhang Xiaobai.

What Don't We Know?

Victoria recorded details about the hospital in her reports, but she didn't talk about herself. Many questions remain about her personal life. What were Victoria's thoughts and feelings about everything she experienced? When did her father and brother die? The executive of the Woman's Missionary Society approved sending a letter of sympathy to Victoria in October 1936. Was this to express regret about Sing Noon's death? Or perhaps this was when Wilson died?

International barriers and language differences can make it difficult to speak to the people who might be able to answer questions about Victoria's son. How old was he when she adopted him? Did they spend a lot of time together when he was growing up? Does Victoria have any grandchildren?

Much of Victoria's story was lost not long after she died. Soldiers raided homes searching for evidence of disloyalty to the Communist government, so friends and family destroyed many of her documents. Victoria's story has been hidden ever since.

A Sister Story

Joan Bamford
Fletcher

At the end of World War II, as Victoria Cheung waited in South China for her fellow missionaries to return to Kongmoon (present-day Jiangmen), Joan Bamford Fletcher accepted a mission in Indonesia. In 1945, on the Indonesian island of Sumatra, there were almost two thousand women and children in the Bangkinang prison camp who needed a safe escort to the coast. For three years the prisoners had suffered the brutal discipline of the camp and endured forced labour, malnutrition and tropical diseases.

Joan's assignment, already hard enough, was made even more difficult by the fact that at the end of the World War II, Indonesia was in chaos. For centuries the country, known as the Dutch East Indies, had been ruled by the Netherlands. During the war, Japanese troops had occupied the country and put all Dutch and Allied soldiers in prison camps, along with almost one hundred thousand civilians.

When the war ended, Indonesian nationalists seized the opportunity to declare their independence as a country. Japan had surrendered, and those in the camps were no longer prisoners of war. Yet it would be dangerous for the prisoners — most of them Dutch — to be released onto an island in the midst of a struggle for independence from the Netherlands. Someone needed to safely escort the people in the camps to freedom, but many soldiers were already deployed elsewhere, and it would take time for them to get to Indonesia.

Joan Bamford Fletcher of Regina, Saskatchewan, was asked to take on this dangerous assignment. She was already in Asia, volunteering in Singapore as a member of the First Aid Nursing Yeomanry, an organization of women highly trained in motor mechanics, first aid, codes and signals. She was promoted to the honorary status of lieutenant and ordered to travel to the Bangkinang camp in the middle of the Sumatran jungle. Once there, she was to transport the prisoners across the island to the coast where they could be taken to safety.

Few records are available about Joan's mission in Indonesia. If it were not for the letters that she wrote home, we would not know much about those six weeks she spent in the jungle, and there is not much information about her life before that.

Joan grew up on a small horse ranch outside of Regina, but even her birthdate has been lost. It is sometimes listed as 1915 or 1918, but a ship's passenger list from November 1910 has baby Joan on a boat to England with her parents and her older sister Madge. So was Joan born in 1910?

We do know that on October 5, 1945, Joan marched into the Japanese military headquarters on the island of Sumatra and announced that she required the assistance of the officers. She was assigned a fleet of trucks, a Japanese-American soldier named Sergeant Art Miyazawa to serve as her interpreter, an officer named Lieutenant Daisaburo Matsuo, who would command the Japanese troops, and forty armed soldiers — none of whom would have been used to taking orders from a volunteer, much less a woman who just weeks before would have been considered an enemy.

With only fifteen vehicles, Joan realized that she could not evacuate all the prisoners at once, so she planned to take 180 at a time, setting off with the first convoy long before the sun rose on October 12, 1945. The journey to the coast was a difficult one. The road took them over 1500-metre-high mountains, at least one partially blown-up bridge, and hairpin turns that became even more perilous in the mud as the rainy season set in. If Joan had been travelling alone, she could have made each journey in eight hours. Instead it took up to twelve. She needed to schedule a five-minute break for her passengers once every hour, and some of them were so weak that they had to be lifted into and out of the trucks. Joan's motor mechanics training was often an advantage as she responded to seemingly constant vehicle breakdowns and flat tires due to the rough mountain roads.

At one of the rivers, there was a wooden trestle bridge that was not sturdy enough to carry heavy military trucks. When the convoy arrived at this crossing, the passengers had to climb out of the vehicles and cross the bridge on foot. Soldiers followed with stretchers carrying those who were not strong enough to walk. Once everyone was safely across, each of the eight empty passenger vehicles rumbled over, the bridge bending and swaying under the weight. The heavy baggage trucks were transported across the river by raft.

The entire crossing took two hours and meant that Joan and the former prisoners did not arrive at the coast until about 6 p.m. Many evenings Joan and her officers unloaded their passengers and then immediately began the long journey back. When they finally had a chance to sleep, it was only for a few hours and on bare, hard boards with nothing but a blanket.

We know that Joan was badly injured on one of the journeys. But was she fixing a truck when it was bumped from behind, as she told her sister? Or was she mowed down by a reckless driver, as Lieutenant Matsuo reported? Either way, Joan was nearly killed when a wheel rolled over her heel, catching her coat and dragging her under the truck. She emerged with a 10-centimetre-long slice to her forehead and scalp. Although Joan allowed a doctor to stop the bleeding, pull the wound together, and bandage it, within two hours she insisted on continuing the evacuation. She would wait until the end of the day to be properly stitched up.

That event was the first of several that earned Joan the respect of all in the unit. She never passed a Japanese soldier after that without him saluting her. On the next convoy, one of the colonels made a special trip to meet Joan. After saying he was sorry about her accident, he asked if there was anything else she needed. "Four more trucks," she said. And he found them for her.

Joan ran the evacuations for three weeks before British troops arrived to take over, at which point she struck up a deal with the brigadier in charge. If he would allow her to continue her mission, she would make sure his general knew nothing about it. In the end, Joan made the crossing all twenty-two times, completing twenty of the trips within the first thirty days.

As the evacuations continued, Indonesian

nationalists grew to be more of a challenge. Many of them had weapons and had received Japanese military training. They barricaded the roads with oil drums and poles, intending to force the convoys to stop. But Joan refused to slow down. She repaired additional trucks she found in the prison compound and increased her fleet to about twenty-five vehicles. She also borrowed a Jeep so that she could better patrol the full length of the convoy, and she adapted the front truck into a crash car to smash through the barricades. She now had an increased guard of seventy Japanese soldiers, and their vehicles had machine guns mounted on top.

Still, her second-last journey proved almost fatal. There are several variations to this story as well, but all of them are similarly intense. When a tire repair was needed somewhere along the convoy, Joan hurried to help. As she was returning to the front of the line with Sergeant Miyazawa, they noticed a man who they did not recognize stealing one of the front cars. Joan realized that the two Dutch passengers were in trouble. She shouted to Miyazawa to pull the Jeep up to the driver's side of the vehicle. Yanking open the door, she saw that the two passengers were nowhere in sight. Joan yelled at the thief to get out. She left five armed guards in charge and she and Miyazawa set off to find the captured men. Joan, as always, was unarmed.

They found the men in a small house with three Indonesian nationalists. One was questioning them, while another held a revolver and a third waved a large bloody knife. Joan began shouting and cursing at the captors, partially to keep up her own courage. Grabbing the knife, she slashed the ropes binding one of the captives, told him to get moving, and headed for the door, hoping no one would stab her while her back was turned. Outside the hut, Joan saw that the commotion had attracted an intimidating crowd of about five hundred people. She pushed through them and herded the passengers back to the safety of her Jeep.

After the final convoy, at the end of their six-week ordeal, the Japanese soldiers agreed that Joan's courage could not be praised enough, and she was presented with the 300-year-old samurai sword that had belonged to the captain of the Japanese Motor Corps. For her service in the Far East, Lieutenant Joan Bamford Fletcher was also recognized by King George VI as a Member of the Order of the British Empire.

By the time Joan returned home to Canada with her samurai sword and award, she also had a plastic jaw. Joan had been in England when complications arose resulting from the malaria she had contracted in the jungle. She required surgery to have many of her lower teeth extracted and part of her bottom jaw removed and rebuilt.

After Joan recovered, she took a position with the British Embassy in Warsaw, Poland. She was posted with the Information Section, and was in charge of the news sheet, the *Voice of England*. Joan may have had additional responsibilities, but they were not the kind of activities she could discuss in letters home.

Foreign newspapers began shutting down, and Joan experienced government censorship at the *Voice of England*. Some of her colleagues began disappearing, and Joan noticed a mysterious car following her. Sometimes she would return to her room and realize that it had been searched while she was out.

One day the phone rang and Joan picked up the receiver to hear a warning that the secret police were coming for her. She had to get out.

She raced home and destroyed her address book before she received notification that the British Royal Air Force would be flying her out. Joan would later tell a reporter that she took nothing through customs except for a nightdress, a tooth brush and Aspirins she had taken to settle her stomach. And she added that she later learned she had evaded arrest by only an hour. Joan was suspected of helping one of her former colleagues at the British Embassy attempt to smuggle a Polish woman out of the country. Under interrogation, he had already given Joan's name.

But Polish diplomats in Ottawa denied that there had been plans for Joan's arrest. The records are sealed, and the Official Secrets Act prevents anyone from discussing her involvement.

The apparent end of Joan's story only leaves more questions. What happened to her after she returned home to Canada? With her guts and tenacity, did she move on to other exploits as a secret

operative? Even her family does not know. Joan's story, like Victoria Cheung's, is hidden under a cloak of secrecy.

Joan Bamford Fletcher died in 1979 and her ashes were scattered in the Pacific Ocean. After her death, Art Miyazawa reported to Joan's sister that, in a fitting final tribute, the Japanese troops she had commanded on Sumatra had added her name to their unit's honour roll of deceased veterans. Joan's samurai sword is preserved at the Canadian War Museum in Ottawa, and a documentary, *Rescue from Sumatra*, was made about her mission in Indonesia. Only a single copy remains available to view. It is on an old video cassette tape and requires a trip to Library and Archives Canada in Ottawa. While Joan's story leaves us with many questions, what little we do know is in danger of being lost.

She Resisted

Mona Parsons

September 29, 1941
Laren, the Netherlands

It was 7 p.m. when the knock on the door finally came. Mona had been expecting it. She had been told that some of her friends had been arrested in the last three days. Many were soon to face a firing squad. This evening Mona needed to put on a performance for the Gestapo, the German secret police. She needed to convince them that her husband, Willem, was away on a fishing trip, not off in hiding, and that she was an innocent Canadian.

She could not let them know that ever since German forces had occupied the Netherlands, she and her husband had been part of a resistance group to help the Allies — countries such as Britain, Poland, France and Canada that were united against Germany. Mona and Willem had been helping to smuggle fallen airmen out of the Netherlands. They sheltered them in their home outside of Amsterdam until the men could move on to a safe house in Leiden and then to the coast where they would be taken away by a British submarine.

Little did Mona know that Richard Pape, one of the navigators that she and Willem had helped to rescue, had just been captured. German officers had found the Leiden safe house and, although Pape had rushed to flush away the pages of his code book and diary, he had forgotten about Mona's calling card in his pocket. When the officers found him, they also found the card and were alerted to Mona's involvement in his escape.

Walking down the hall, Mona caught sight of herself in the mirror. Did she look nervous? She told herself the same thing she had told Willem before he went into hiding: with all her training as an actress, she could play this role. She pinned back a rogue curl and crossed the foyer to open the door.

Mona greeted the officers using one of the few German phrases she knew. "*Meine herren.*" Gentlemen.

She invited them in for brandy and cigars. In the solarium, the men allowed themselves to be amused by her act but they were not fooled. Within an hour they marched Mona out to a waiting car, denying her requests for her coat, and they took her to Weteringschans prison in Amsterdam for interrogation.

Mona's guards were certain she would break — they

were masters of threats, humiliation and bullying. But Mona would never give up Willem. She derived her strength from knowing he was free.

For three months Mona was confined to a cold cell with nothing but a straw mattress and a bucket for her waste until the morning of December 22. At 8 a.m. her cell door opened and Mona was told to get dressed. Though she did not know it at the time, Willem had been arrested and she was now of no use to the Nazis. Mona was driven to the Carlton Hotel where the Germans, furious at her defiance, would make her stand trial in front of a military court, a situation unheard of for a woman. She felt the bottom fall out of her world. Mona did not have a lawyer. She had not even been informed of the charges against her.

That morning was a blur. Mona's assigned counsel spoke no English or Dutch and, although she requested a new lawyer, he was given no time to explain what was going on. Mona resolved that she would not break down in front of the court. Shortly after the trial started, the judge asked Mona to stand. As he spoke, Mona understood a single word. *"Todesstrafe."* Death penalty. Her case had already been decided. Mona was to be executed by firing squad.

She fought to retain her composure. Putting her heels together in the style of a German soldier, she respectfully bid the court good day. *"Guten morgen, meine herren."*

But as she was escorted from the room, the judge approached to shake her hand.

"My dear woman," he said. "You are very brave. I recommend that you appeal this sentence."

Twenty-eight days later, Mona was instead sentenced to life in prison at hard labour. She was taken to the railway station to catch the train that would transport her to Anrath Penitentiary in Germany. While she waited in the office, German guards marched in with three prisoners. There was something about the thin man by the window that made Mona look twice. He had dyed his hair and changed his appearance, but Mona recognized her husband. She ran to him and was only able to tell him to have courage before the guards tore them apart.

Mona spent the next four years in penitentiary after

penitentiary, transferred from one to the next in airless cattle cars crammed full of other women. Living with thieves and murderers, she slept with three other prisoners in a cell built for one, always with a stinking waste bucket in the middle of the room. The squalid conditions resulted in coughing, vomiting and diarrhea that often lasted for months.

Forced to toil in support of the German war effort, Mona sabotaged everything she could. When she constructed bomb igniters, she found ways to mis-wire them. And when Mona was made to knit for the German army after bronchitis put an end to her factory work, she made sure to stitch a rebellious knot into the sole of each sock. It was her little way of making sure to bring suffering to the soldier who would wear it.

In 1945 Mona was moved to Vechta prison in Germany. Through the barred windows of the women's building, she could see the men's prison and the airstrip. There was also a German military hospital on site. Working in the kitchen, Mona often delivered provisions to patients in the hospital, to the officers and to prisoners in solitary confinement. Whenever she could, she smuggled pieces of potato back to her cellmates in a pocket she had sewn into her uniform. Her small rebellions, singing songs or finding ways to lift the spirits of her fellow inmates, ensured she was often punished with time in isolation from the other prisoners.

Shortly after Mona arrived at Vechta, another group of prisoners was delivered. The guards were warned that one of the women, a twenty-two-year-old baroness named Wendelien van Boetzelaer, had tried to escape twice before. She was placed in one of the solitary confinement cells on the top floor. Determined to escape Vechta, Mona knew the baroness had invaluable experience that could help her — if only the two women could talk to one another.

Having done her own share of time in isolation, Mona knew the best way to make an ally. When she slipped half a potato through the bars of Wendy's cell, the baroness gratefully became her friend.

Mona had also found that if the director of the prison was approached privately, she was often sympathetic to her prisoners. At Mona's request, she granted permission for Wendy to leave her cell to work, exercise and take meals. It was enough for Mona and Wendy to find brief moments in which they could plan their escape. They convinced the director to give them each a sweater and warm shoes that had been taken from the women when they arrived. Both prisoners secretly agreed that they would escape when the first opportunity arose.

On the frosty morning of March 24, 1945, the women were headed to work when the prison and airstrip were attacked. Mona watched as a cluster of Allied bombs fell on the men's prison. The building was destroyed and everyone inside was killed. As the female prisoners and guards dropped to the ground, Mona was surprised to hear the director give the order to open the gates. Did she know of the escape plan and sympathize? Or was she resigned to the thought that the prison would fall?

Either way, she looked at the women and told them they could take their chances with the bombs — or with guards' bullets.

Wendy and Mona chose the bullets. Hand in hand, they ran into the smoke and gunfire. They did not stop even when they reached the end of the airstrip. By nightfall they were almost 20 kilometres from Vechta. Having buried their prison aprons, they now wore the plain clothes given to them by the director and they hoped to pass for Germans.

They were starving and cold. Hiding out in a barn, Mona realized they had a further problem. After four years in German prisons, she could now speak the language, but she had a heavy accent. It would give them away.

"If we get caught, this time we'll be shot," Wendy said. "We will have to pretend that you are a little gaga and that you cannot speak properly."

The women walked for three weeks, doing farm chores in exchange for food and somewhere to sleep. After their shoes fell apart, they continued barefoot. Their feet were soon covered with infected sores and blisters. Weakened by malnourishment, Mona could not fight off the infection. It entered her blood and was carried to the rest of her body. Still she kept walking.

At the Dutch border, Allied forces were pushing the German troops back into Germany. There was no safe place for Mona and Wendy to hide together. Local farmers shared their homes, but the women were sent to farms that were more than 2 kilometres apart. Mona now had to keep up her act without Wendy to speak for her. She shared a bed with the farmers' twelve-year-old daughter and was petrified that she would give herself away by talking in her sleep.

Now that she was so close to the Netherlands, Mona was tortured by the thought of having to wait out the attacks. During a lull in the fighting, the farmer took food to a young soldier in his field. From the doorway, Mona heard the crack of a shell and saw a plume of smoke as the two men were blown to pieces. Shaken, she ran to join the rest of the family in the cellar. She waited three days until the first wave of Allied troops had pushed through. Mona did not know then that Canadian soldiers were close behind them.

When the fighting moved on, Mona continued walking, now alongside families who were also fleeing. As she crossed into the Netherlands, the war-torn countryside shocked her but it could not put a damper on her spirits.

Now in Allied-liberated territory, there were soldiers who could help her.

Mona made her way to the closest battalion and introduced herself. But she was greeted with suspicion. Here was a woman who, at 173 centimetres tall, was so sick that she now weighed only 39 kilograms. Mona was draped in rags, matted in dirt, and yet she claimed to own an estate near Amsterdam. Her story did not ring true, and the soldiers had been warned to beware of female German spies.

"But I'm Canadian," Mona told them.

"Then where are you from?"

"A little village in Nova Scotia," Mona said. "Wolfville."

"My goodness," one soldier said, looking around at the others. "We are the North Nova Scotia Highlanders and I'm from Halifax."

Mona was taken to the Canadian Army Rear Head-quarters in Oldenburg where she would have to prove her identity. There she met several more soldiers from Nova Scotia, including Major General Harry Foster. Harry was a childhood friend of Mona's from Wolfville. He was shocked to see her, but he was happy to vouch for her. Mona was given medical care, a bed among the nurses, food — and even three Moirs chocolates that had been sent from Nova Scotia. Someone found her some paper so that she could write home to her parents.

After she returned to Laren, Mona was relieved to hear that Wendy was safe and that Willem had been liberated from a concentration camp. He would be home soon.

Mona received citations for bravery from the British Air Force and the U.S. Army. She spent much of the next few years travelling with Willem and nursing him through sickness after sickness. Willem's death in 1956 was hard on Mona. She learned that he had left part of his estate to another woman who had been their close friend for years. The final insult came when Willem's son from his first marriage reappeared to claim the rest of the inheritance.

Mona returned to Nova Scotia and moved to Halifax, where she once again met up with Harry Foster. They were married in 1959, but Harry died five years later. Mona returned to Wolfville in 1969. She became known as a somewhat eccentric old lady who loved exchanging ideas with young people and listening to them play her piano. When Mona died of pneumonia in 1976, she was buried in the Parsons' family plot in Wolfville. The inscription on the headstone reads:

Mona L. Parsons
1901–1976
Wife of
Major General
H. W. Foster
C.B.E. D.S.O.

No mention is made of Mona's own commendations for bravery, and Harry himself is buried with his first wife in a cemetery 15 kilometres away.

A more fitting memorial is the bronze sculpture erected in 2017 near the site of the Wolfville cenotaph. Entitled "The joy is almost too much to bear," it echoes words Mona wrote to her parents on the day the Netherlands was liberated. In it, a thin figure kicks up her clogs and dances, expressing Mona's irrepressible joy and unfailing spirit in the face of the most daunting adversity.

How Do We Know What We Know?

After the war, when Mona arrived at the Canadian General Hospital in the Netherlands, she was given a pen and paper, and she immediately began a thirty-four-page letter to her parents, telling them much of her story. A journalist named Allan Kent accompanied Mona when she returned to her home in Laren and wrote a series of articles about her. There are also documents that survive from the war — among them is a list of prisoners being transferred to Anrath Penitentiary in 1942 that includes Mona's name, and letters that Mona was allowed to send from Wiedenbruck prison. In 2000, some of the people who remembered Mona — including her old friend Wendelien, the baroness — were interviewed for a documentary called *The Canadians: Mona Parsons*.

Andria Hill-Lehr's book *Mona Parsons: From Privilege to Prison, from Nova Scotia to Nazi Europe* examines Mona's life growing up and her experiences before the war.

What Do We Know?

Mona studied acting at the Acadia Ladies' Seminary in Wolfville, Nova Scotia. There are photos of her in the Ziegfeld Follies, a famous New York musical production.

In the Netherlands, Mona and Willem's large estate still stands in Laren. In it is the attic where they hid Allied airmen. A "closet door" disguised a secret staircase leading up to a space that was more comfortable than many other people in

hiding would have had. There were beds, a private bathroom, windows, a radio — and even chocolate.

When the baroness was interviewed, she recalled that Mona was a woman with a rebellious spirit. She lifted the mood of other prisoners by sharing recipes or by singing happy songs, military songs — even naughty songs!

What Don't We Know?

We know that Mona was imprisoned in Anrath, Wiedenbruck and Vechta. But where was she between Anrath and Wiedenbruck? At the end of the war, many official documents were lost. Without knowing where Mona was held, it's difficult to know where to start looking for more information.

We know nothing about the director at Vechta who threw open the prison gates during the bombing. Why would she take such a risk? We don't even know her name.

With no memorial until 2017, Mona's story wasn't recognized as something that should be preserved. At the end of her life, in order to pay for medical expenses, Mona sold her possessions — including the piano and other valuable pieces of history that had been in her home during the war. These exhibits were scattered instead of archived, bought by people who may have no idea of what they possess. The biggest challenge, as Andria Hill-Lehr says, is "pulling Mona's story back together again."

Acknowledgements

Admiration and thanks to my husband Marc LaBerge who somehow never seems to tire of kid wrangling, wordsmithing, holding me up and talking me down. This two-and-a-half-year labour of love would have been twice as long without you.

A world of pizza and road trips to Ethan, Nat and Dani for their patience all those days I was locked away in my "Plotting Shed," and for their infectious excitement that kept me fired up even through the most challenging moments of this project. I wrote this for you and other readers like you.

Thanks to my editors Anne Shone, who believed in *Fierce* from the beginning, and Tamara Sztainbok, who invested mad hours of research and asked all the hard questions — and wasn't afraid of the answers. Willow Dawson has gifted this book with her own bold spirit along with the essence of each woman, expressed so thoughtfully in her evocative illustrations. Thanks too to art director, Andrea Casault and to the entire team at Scholastic Canada.

To Patricia McCormack for sharing her insightful articles on Ttha'naltther, to Andria Hill-Lehr for her unfailing dedication to Mona Parsons, to John Price for his work on Victoria Cheung, and to Lawrence Barkwell for his writing on Charlotte Small — for all the phone calls and emails, I express my deepest gratitude to each of you. David Bouchard, Arlene Chan, Natasha Henry, Julie Mercredi and Suzanne Methot, readers who generously shared their cultural knowledge and experience, who thoughtfully answered questions and added to the depth and the reach of this book, you have my heartfelt appreciation.

Thank you also to the fierce and fabulous librarians who

assisted with this project, especially Pat Kermath, Penny Presswood, Kathy Bouma, Rebecca Hine, Joyce Tenhage, Brittany Tenhage, Robin Cooper, Robin Sakowski, Frances Theilade and the ever-resourceful Deanna Stevens, who tackled and triumphed over every challenge I posed.

And this book would not exist without the research skills of the enthusiastic archivists Peggy D'Orsay, Vivian Belik, Linda Johnson, Deb Blackie, Blair Galston, Emily Sommers, Heather Gardiner, Margery Hadley and the staff of the Provincial Archives of Saskatchewan. As well I'd like to thank Brenda Rogers, Carol Cooney and Trevor Schubert for creating, preserving and sharing such an extensive family archive about Catherine and Augustus Schubert; and Jean Little and Pat de Vries for inviting me into their home to share their mother's memories and photos of Victoria Cheung.

A huge shout-out to fellow writers who offered early critiques or advice: Joel Sutherland, Marsha Skrypuch, Kira Vermond, Jean Mills, Helaine Becker, Claire Eamer, Gillian Chan, Natalie Hyde, Suzanne Del Rizzo and Eric Walters; to friends who offered support and the odd kick in the butt: Shauna Hanna, Crysten Miller, Mel Hartzell and Lynn Crocker; and to those who offered their homes during the most intense periods of research and editing, Cara LaBerge and Steve Gibson, and Joanne Levy and Deke Snow.

And thanks to my parents, Ian and Sandra Dalrymple — the only people who can say they've been behind every book I've written since I was ten. And at least this one you didn't have to produce on your typewriter, Mum.

Publisher's Note

The women included in this book, from different times and different backgrounds, were chosen because their achievements, courage and strength were truly remarkable. These are not the only stories, nor are they complete. We hope *Fierce* is the beginning of a conversation. It's an invitation to consider the many lives that have been lived off the pages of history books, and a reminder that all history is story and interpretation, alongside fact — all of which require careful research and critical thinking.

Our sincere gratitude goes to the expert reviewers who shared their time and knowledge so these stories could be told.

A Note on Names

Sometimes the names commonly used for Indigenous groups are not the same as the traditional names that people use to refer to themselves. We have chosen the words people use to refer to themselves wherever possible. For example, instead of Cree, we use Nehiyawak; instead of Athapaskan we use Dene; instead of Shuswap we use the term Secwepemc.

Similarly, names for individuals are often recorded and handed down through history in a variety of ways. Wherever possible, we have chosen to use the spelling each woman used herself. Lucile Hunter spelled her name with one *L* on official correspondence, and the Yukon Archives list her legal name as Lucile. But her gravestone and various sources record her name as Lucille. Victoria Cheung signed her letters to the Woman's Missionary Society with an *E* in her last name, and yet her name is often recorded as Chung. Although Ttha'naltther's name is often recorded in books as Thanadelthur, we use the spelling preferred by the Dene elders who pass down her story from generation to generation.